S0-CFF-837

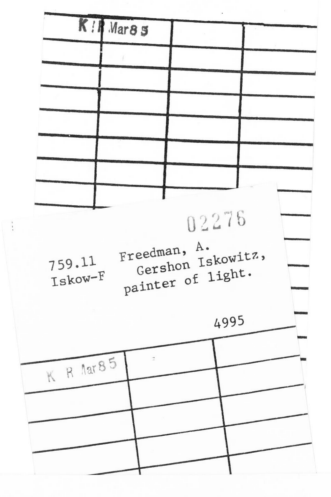

Date Due

K!R Mar8 5			

02276

4995

K R Mar8 5	:	

02276

6/He

GERSHON ISKOWITZ : PAINTER OF LIGHT

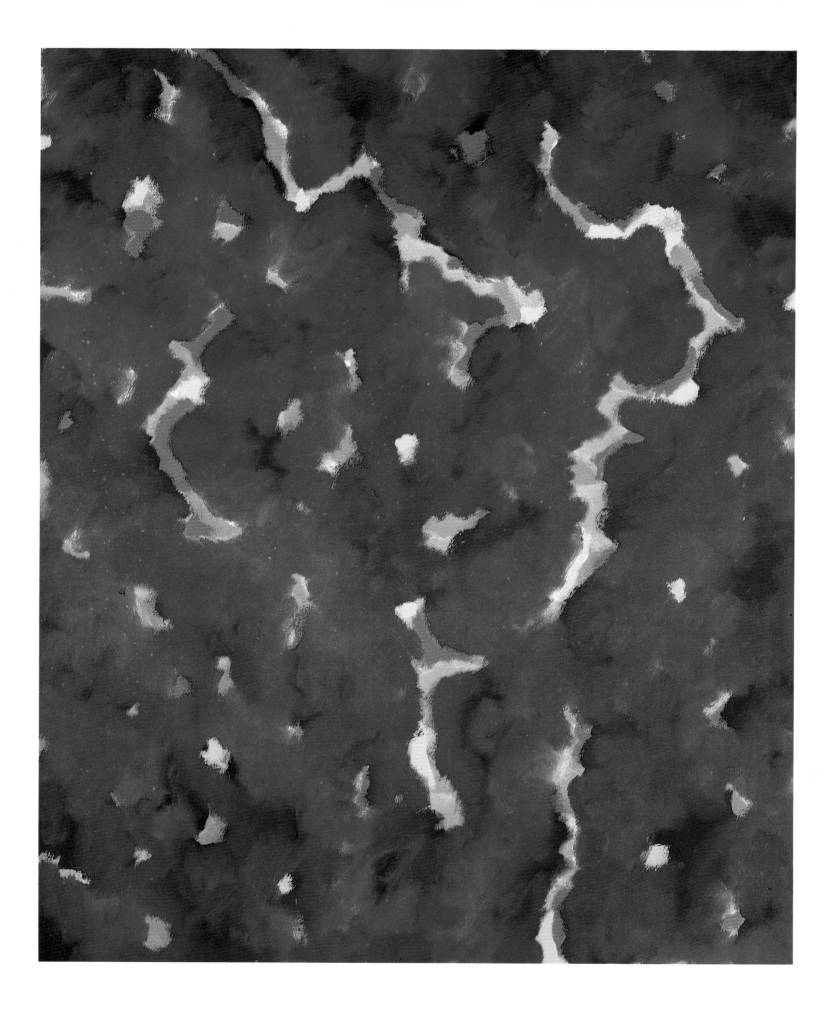

Adele Freedman

GERSHON ISKOWITZ
PAINTER OF LIGHT

MERRITT PUBLISHING COMPANY LIMITED
Toronto / Vancouver

Text: © Adele Freedman 1982
Illustrations: © Gallery Moos Limited 1982

Published by Merritt Publishing Company Limited,
Toronto / Vancouver.

Distributed in Canada by John Wiley and Sons
Canada Limited

Canadian Cataloguing in Publication Data

Freedman, Adele.
Gershon Iskowitz: painter of light

Bibliography: p.
Includes index.
ISBN 0-920886-16-7

1. Iskowitz, Gershon. 2. Painters – Canada – Biography.
I. Title: Gershon Iskowitz: painter of light.

ND249.I85F73   759.11   C82–094147–6

This book is published in co-operation with
Gallery Moos Limited, Toronto.

1 *Night Blues B*   1981
oil on canvas
116.2 × 99.1 cm

For DEVORAH ISKOWITZ, 1925–1942

CONTENTS

PREFACE

I first met Gershon Iskowitz in October 1977 when a friend suggested I interview him for an art column I was starting in *Toronto Life*. I walked up the two flights of stairs to his studio on Spadina Avenue one evening, like the proverbial *tabula rasa*, hoping as only a fledgling critic can that Iskowitz would do the rest. He did not disappoint me. The thick steel door swung open and a vigorous-looking man with mischievous eyes and nervous hands welcomed me with a loud 'hello.' Moments later I was seated with a shot of vodka in my hand listening to Iskowitz's unstoppable flow of anecdotes and free-association. Every so often he punctuated his remarks by pulling out a canvas and talking about how he paints and thinks. Before I had a chance to submit completely to his unique brand of hypnotism, he suggested we go over to La Cantinetta Restaurant for another drink. There he continued spinning his stories, breaking into Yiddish at the punch lines and reliving his childhood in Poland with gusto.

After filling in the blanks by studying the Iskowitz file at Gallery Moos, I wrote my piece and submitted it for publication. The next day the checker at the magazine phoned me distraught. 'We can't go ahead,' she said. 'Iskowitz denied everything. Whenever I asked him to verify a quote, he insisted it was just a joke.' The article was published nonetheless and a year afterward, when I saw Isko-witz again at Gallery Moos, he told me how much he had liked it and suggested we get together for dinner.

That was the beginning of a long series of dinners and visits to his studio, where he showed me works in progress and offered his opinions about everything from art to borscht. As a special treat he would dive into the storage area and pull out an old canvas, a sixties skyscape, or his portfolio of concentration camp drawings, exclaiming, 'Hey, have I ever shown you this?' Every time I thought I had seen everything in his studio, out would come some other painting or drawing. I had begun to review exhibitions for the *Globe and Mail* at the end of 1978 and Isko-witz's whirlwind comments about painting and the art world helped me enormously in understanding what it was I was looking at. He also encouraged me in my writing, reading everything I published and counselling me never to give up the fight. Continuity was the most important thing, he said, followed closely by clarity of expression. I learned as much about writing from him as I did about painting.

Sometime in 1980, after the Art Gallery of Ontario had notified him about his forty-year retrospective, Iskowitz suggested I write a book about him. At first I hesitated, thinking he would eventually deny everything he said anyway. I agreed to start taping his story for eventual publication on one condition – that he would not hold back anything or tell me what to leave out. He agreed. During the summer of 1980 we met once every two weeks or so, generally over dinner at La Cantinetta, to record his life. When I played back the tapes in September I was very moved. That someone who had endured such distress and fragmentation could think so positively about life made me feel humble. I found it wonderful that he could be inspired by the flutter of leaves and the breaking of clouds to the point where he based an entire body of work on such random acts of nature. Here was a man who had learned to take nothing for granted.

There are not many people who are intimate with Iskowitz, but I learned a great deal about him from Dorothy Cameron, his first dealer, and Walter Moos, his present one. Moos was always at the other end of the telephone when I needed him. I spoke with the three young artists who claim to have been influenced by him, David Bolduc, Dan Solomon, and John MacGregor; with Bert and Elena Weir who welcomed him to McKellar; and with William Coryell, who first took him there. Luigi Orgera told me about his friendship with Iskowitz and offered his insights. William Atkinson, the president of Merritt Publishing, arranged a screening of the two films made about Iskowitz, *Standing Apart* and *I Paint What I Know*. Gerard Jennings

and Ken Forsyth at Gallery Moos supplied slides and moral support. My editor, Rosemary Shipton, made sure I said what I meant, and H.J. Kirchhoff scoured the proofs. For those chapters dealing with Iskowitz's experiences in the camps I relied on Lucy Dawidowicz's authoritative work, *The War Against the Jews* 1933–1945; every detail of Iskowitz's testimony checked out. Most of all I am indebted to Iskowitz himself for sharing his memories with me and allowing me into his present.

GERSHON ISKOWITZ : PAINTER OF LIGHT

1 THE ARTIST

The Gershon Iskowitz Retrospective mounted by the Art Gallery of Ontario in January 1982 honours a remarkable crossover figure. Iskowitz spent his childhood and adolescence in Kielce, a small town in western Poland, his early manhood in Auschwitz and Buchenwald, and the years since 1949 in Toronto. During all that time there was scarcely one day in which he did not draw, sketch, or paint. His reputation rests on two principal achievements: his singular and exemplary dedication to painting; and a body of work tied to the Canadian landscape so much more impassioned than the standard version handed down by the Group of Seven that it is almost erotic by comparison.

A loner by nature and inclination, Iskowitz has never conformed to the prevailing art idioms of his day or belonged to a self-congratulatory clique. In his view art should not pay court to fashion; and he chooses to define fashion as any style engaged in by more than one person at any given time. When acrylics became popular, he resolutely stuck by his oils. Rollers, spatulas, rotors, and glue form no part of his studio inventory: to this day he uses bristle brushes, an upright canvas, tubes of paint, and a palette. He does not believe that experimenting in mixed media – a few paintings here, a sculpture or two there, a foray into photography – can do anything for an artist,

with the possible exception of Picasso, other than divert him from his purpose. At the mention of any *ism* beloved of art historians he is likely to shrug his shoulders and utter a spontaneous string of pronouncements on the lines of: 'In society everyone is supposed to be the same. You are supposed to paint in a certain style that's fashionable. You don't do that. You're on your own.'

Since painting for this natural artist is the total expression of his life, his philosophy of life, and his lifestyle, he considers his retrospective nothing less than a personal vindication. During the many long months of its preparation he began to look forward to it with the same mixture of pride and dread felt by Jews approaching the Day of Atonement, when God makes known his judgment on the personal worth of each of his followers. Iskowitz's values and attitudes are embedded in each of the hundred-odd paintings and drawings in the exhibition, loaned by the National Gallery, the Art Bank, provincial galleries, American museums, and a variety of private and corporate collections. They trace a forty-year journey which began in Europe and reached its destination high above the clouds in the Canadian north.

The earliest work, dated September 1941, is a pen-and-ink drawing done the day the Nazis liquidated Iskowitz's hometown; the most recent, three large-scale oil paintings completed in 1981, are stunning examples of his mature style – aerial views of the landscape exploding with colour and emotion. The paintings and drawings in between are stations on the road from figuration to abstraction, although Iskowitz himself refuses to call his paintings abstract. 'They're real,' he once protested to writer and filmmaker Peter Mellen. 'They're very, very much real. I see those things.'

His progress through the Canadian landscape has gone through perceptible transformations, however, or as he himself has noticed, 'Transitions come every five or six years.' In the mid-fifties, when he first went out sketching in the Ontario countryside, he painted 'straight landscapes' but his wild strokes and distortions did not suggest the Canadian landscape people were used to seeing on canvas. 'People said I didn't paint like the Group of Seven,' he has said, 'but when I went north, it didn't *look* like the Group of Seven.' Still it was possible to look at an Iskowitz landscape of the fifties and say with some certainty, 'there's a tree,' or 'there's the moon.' As time went on making those identifications became harder. Searching for ways to relate colour and the landscape in order to express their fluctuating moods and rhythms, he began disintegrating recognizable images – trees, branches, leaves, sunsets – into transparent streaks and patches of coloured light.

The motif of the dot or patch of colour had appeared in his work as early as the late forties where he used it to represent a person's head or body or an article of clothing – a hat, perhaps, or a shoe. The dots reappeared in the idealized views of Kielce he painted in Toronto in 1951 and 1952: they are small concentrations of colour and energy into which he compressed a thousand intuitions about the way reality, both emotional and physical, is structured. He became more and more fascinated by these shapes as he continued on his way, until they completely took over his canvases.

It took years for Iskowitz to break free of the conventions of European landscape painting, however, and he did so with great tact. His large canvas, *Spring*, painted in 1962, clearly portrays a tree but it is a transparent tree caught in a filmy veil of ether. Five years later the trunk of the tree had disappeared and its leaves had been shattered into oval patches of intense shimmering colour floating evenly across the canvas, each invested with the reality and force of nature as Iskowitz felt it. Soon after this breakthrough came his first helicopter trip to the far north, which released him into a new way of seeing. The perspective became one of looking down at nature – or its metaphorical shorthand, the swirling dots – through endless blankets of grey cloud.

'I always thought the first ones really did come out of the landscape,' remarked Dorothy Cameron, Iskowitz's first dealer. 'And then you would see the landscape breaking up and it was like the leaves flying, and the blossoms flying, until you just got these spots of colour. But it all came out of something that was an *explosion* in nature.' Iskowitz would agree, only with an added proviso: as far as he is concerned, everything he has drawn and painted since he was seven is part of one continuum. 'What I do now is part of what I did then,' he has stated. Paradoxically, the further he moved from representational painting, the closer he has come to his roots. 'You know what I think about now, when I paint? I think about my childhood,' he said in 1977; or 'Ontario looks like Poland, the skies and the sunsets. Some parts of Ontario look like the parts where I was born.'

One of the most impressive accomplishments of Iskowitz's art is the way the complexity of his past experiences has been absorbed into the vibrant simplicity of his painting. He resents being thought of only as a nature painter because that seems to imply he is not describing human nature as well. For him the two are a unity. In fact, critics have generally been at a loss to classify Iskowitz's work because it is so personal, or as Dorothy Cameron recalled, 'His painting comes out of his own search. No

one has ever taught Gershon anything.' In a single decade, the seventies, reviewers called him a colour-field painter, an impressionist, and an abstract expressionist. 'I don't believe any of it,' he insists. 'You are what you are. I'm a painter. I paint.'

He never paints during the day, however. That would puncture the elaborate ritual by which he conducts his life and protects his art. Days are reserved for being out in the world, for strolling across Spadina Avenue for a light lunch at the Bagel Restaurant and, after exchanging a few jokes with the owner, following a predetermined route which takes him, first, to his dealer's gallery on Yorkville Avenue to pick up his mail; next, into all the other galleries in the neighbourhood to have a look around; and later on, when dusk has fallen, to another home away from home, La Cantinetta Restaurant. If a woman is joining him for dinner, he invariably presents her with a rose. When the strolling musicians ask for a request, it is always his favourite aria from Bizet's *The Pearl Fishers*. The waiters address him as Maestro; he, in turn, greets all of them by name. After lingering over one last shot of vodka or one last cup of espresso, he sometimes moves on to the Pilot Tavern for more conversation or even to the El Mocambo for a set of rock and roll. 'Gershon can't work with an audience or with anybody else's ideas,' commented his

friend Luigi Orgera, the proprietor of La Cantinetta, 'but he also has to go out and have a drink and talk to people. That winds him up.' Or as Iskowitz would have it, 'Extreme change before you go into painting is good mentally.'

Come 1 AM, without fail, Iskowitz is back in his studio, alone, wound up, ready at last to turn around one of the canvases stacked against the wall and begin to paint. Stripped to a pair of shorts, his radio tuned to CHFI's all-night classical music programme, he paints the night away – a practice he began in 1945 after emerging from a night that was six years long. He paints his memories of the Canadian north – colours and configurations he may have glimpsed years ago from the windows of a helicopter; and at the same time as he is stripping away inessential details in the crucible of his memory he is painting his past. 'At night I can escape,' he once told a reporter. 'I just go into my world, into my memories. Some are pleasant, some dramatic. My mind becomes free.' He paints with passion, grinding his brush into the canvas so hard the hairs become embedded in the paint like bits of stray underbrush. First he covers his entire canvas with patches of colour, working quickly and intuitively. Sometimes he will think about a certain shade of red for three days to have it clear in his mind before mixing his pigments. He never uses

1 *Luigi Orgera*   1980
felt pen
42.5 × 35 cm

2 *Orange B*   1980
oil on canvas
91.4 × 86.4 cm

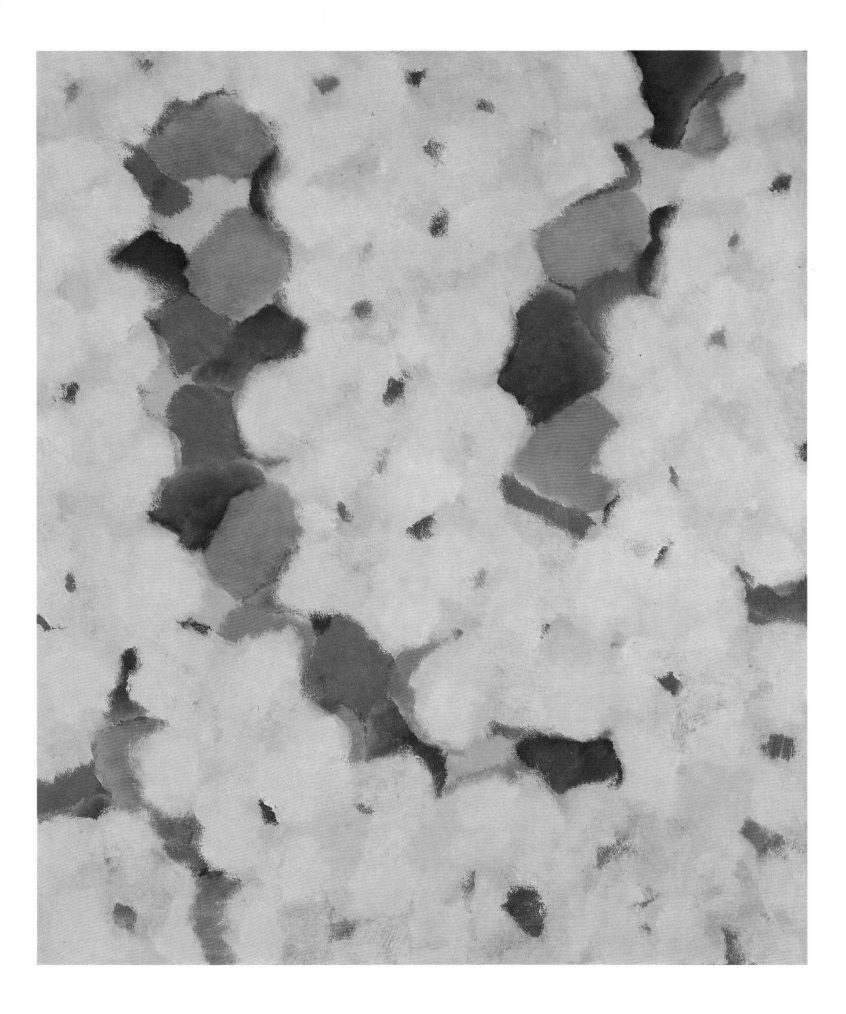

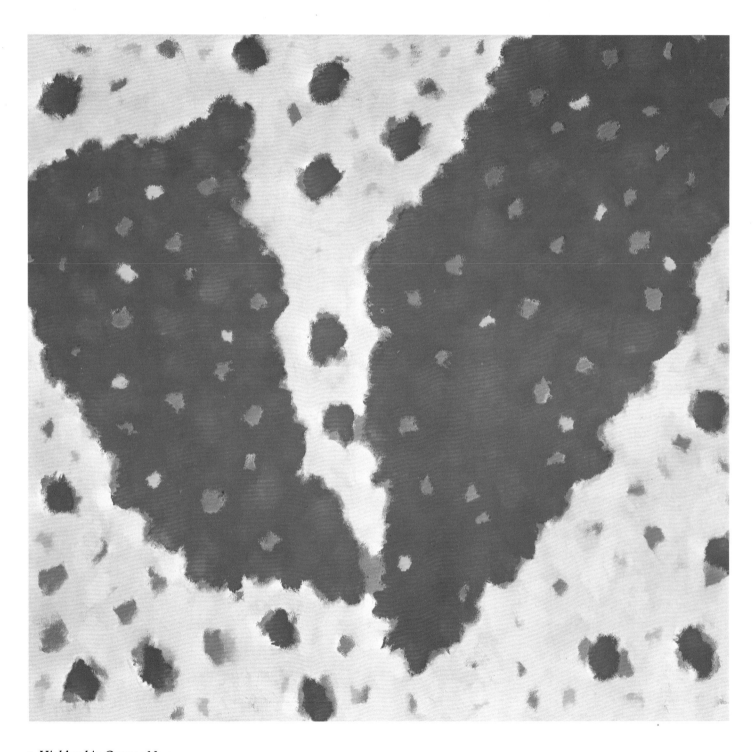

3 *Highland in Orange No 2* 1977
oil on canvas
167.5 × 183 cm

4 *Highland in Green No 2* 1977
oil on canvas
106.7 × 96.5 cm

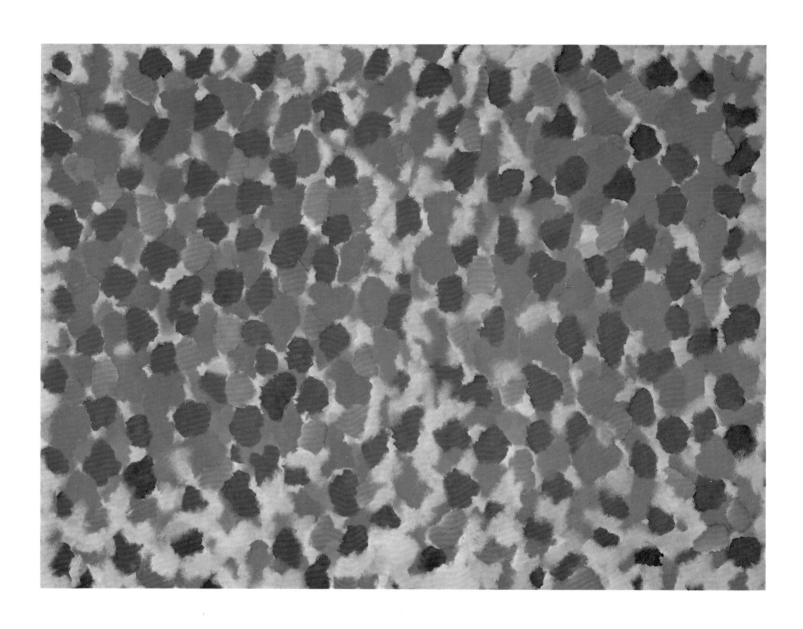

5 *Newscape* 1976
oil on canvas
152 × 208 cm

6 *Red F* 1979
oil on canvas
160 × 137.2 cm

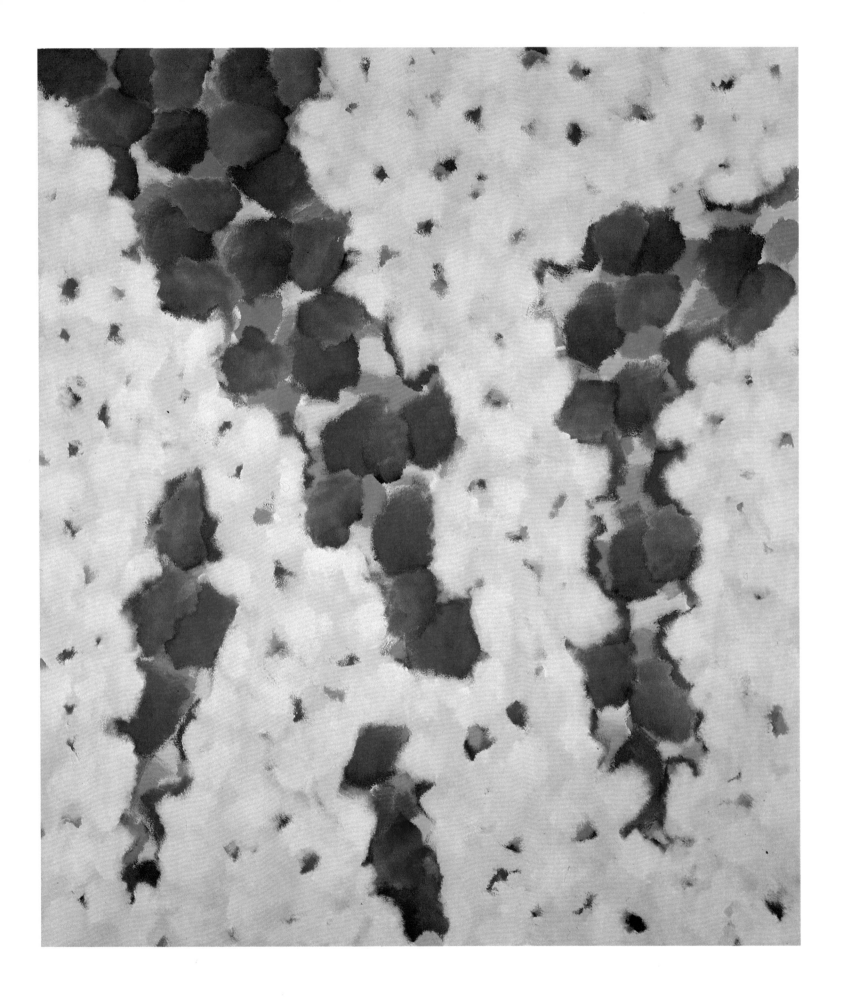

single colours straight from the tube, preferring to create his own. The mere thought of a muddy colour, much less the sight of one, is enough to make him wince. 'Muggy' colours, as he calls them, are in his view a sign of bad mental health. When every nuance of every colour is right, he covers the matrix with a veil of grey or blue or red or green which he models so the colours underneath erupt into motion. This process, or ritual, may go on for weeks.

He paints in series named for the particular colour or ideation of colours he is investigating at the time – midnight blues or orange/reds. 'Gershon is a painter who likes to explore an idea,' said his dealer, Walter Moos. 'He doesn't want to jump from one mode to the next. When Gershon is in a series, he does explore it. There are tremendous subtle variations. I would use the analogy of Monet: it is certainly not true that when you have seen one haystack by Monet, you have seen them all.' For Iskowitz the issue is much simpler. 'I just paint,' he once remarked. 'I paint what I know. I always try to get endless spaces that won't block the eye looking through, so that you wonder what is happening behind the paint. Art is like a mystery. Everything combines together – your social life, your painting, your friends – that's what makes it.'

There are some who see Iskowitz as a Polish Zen monk who lives for his art to the exclusion of everything else.

7 *Deep Red No 6* 1976
oil on canvas
195.6 × 228.6 cm

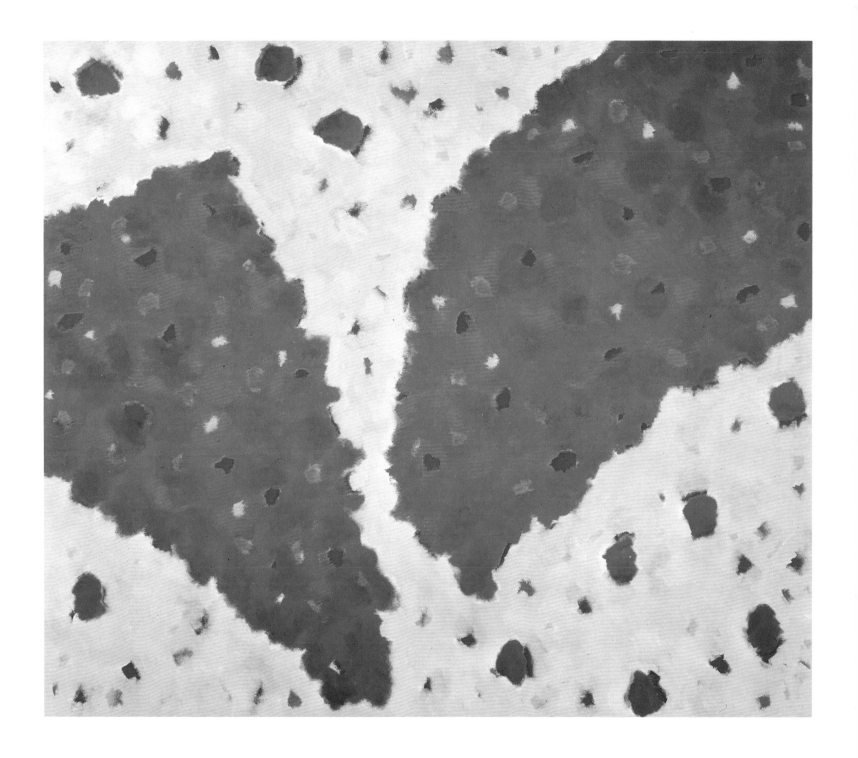

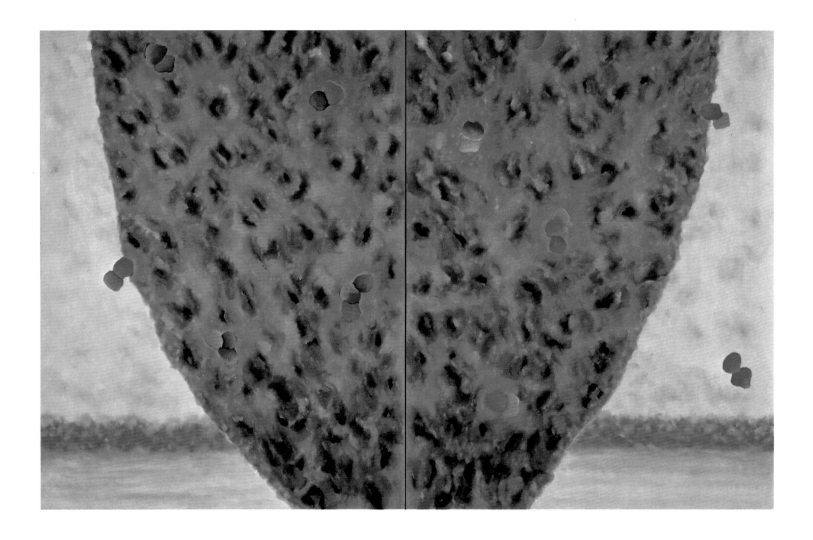

8 *Uplands B* 1969–70
oil on canvas
213.4 × 355.3 cm (diptych)

'He's missed out,' said one observer tersely. 'He's created an artificial environment in which he allows certain things to come in and blocks out the rest.' As an illustration these critics point to the studio he lived and worked in for twenty years after 1962, with its rudimentary furnishings and half-dozen lightbulbs dangling on cords from the ceiling; or his strict schedule, his rule of never taking vacations, his inability to forego a single night of painting, the fact that he is not married. What they fail to appreciate is that Iskowitz does not consider himself deprived. 'I'm really happy when I paint and I'm left alone,' he once told Peter Mellen. 'I live alone but I'm not alone.' He looks uncomfortable on a down-filled sofa but he enjoys good food and drink, good conversation, and clothes made of good cloth. 'He's an innocent man in a sense,' said Orgera. 'He gets fascinated by the simple things of life. There's nothing plastic – everything is real for him.' His only vice is painting; and by clinging to it so obsessively he has fulfilled a dream he has had since he was old enough to remember his dreams.

2 KIELCE

There were not many Jews living in the Polish town of Kielce in the twenties who could afford to go to the movies. The price of admission to a movie theatre would buy two kilos of the best meat or a filling dinner at a restaurant. With the exception of a small professional class, the 18,000 Jews who made up a quarter of the town's population earned a meagre living as shoemakers, pedlars, tailors, and merchants; at least half of them were undernourished. Besides, if the Jews in the ghetto area wished to escape the omnipresent threat of pogroms carried out by the Poles with the approval of the Roman Catholic church and the Fascist government, they did not need help from Hollywood. Hundreds of Yiddish theatre groups were touring Poland in this period, and in Kielce performances took place every Thursday through Sunday night over the winter. The famed Wilna Troupe's production of *The Dybbuk* drew larger crowds than American westerns.

For a nine-year-old Gershon Iskowitz, however, movies were a priority and he quickly figured out a way to see them regularly. One day in 1930 he walked over to the movie theatre a block from his house on the north side of town and made the owner an offer. In exchange for drawing posters of matinée idols, he asked for free admission to one week-night screening and the six-hour Sunday matinée. At first the man was skeptical; but perhaps on account of the boy's persistence or the novelty of his idea, he decided to give him a chance. Gershon hurried back home and set to work on his first poster: Laurel and Hardy. This was not a simple line drawing but a bright watercolour portrait with 'lots of yellows and blues,' built up in layers over a base coat of Chinese white.

During the next three or four years the posters kept coming – Charlie Chaplin, Buster Keaton, and Harold Lloyd, the silent stars of the twenties; followed by Gary Cooper, Wallace Beery, Douglas Fairbanks, Merle Oberon, and Bette Davis, who had become the heroes and heroines in small towns and large cities alike. Gershon studied the movies with the same enthusiasm other boys did the Bible; they were the books in his secular *cheder*. 'I liked everything that made sense, that gave you some knowledge,' he recalls, enumerating some of his favourite films: the first talking *Dr Jekyll and Mr Hyde* with Fredric March, Tom Mix westerns, anything starring Merle Oberon, Chaplin's *City Lights* – films which could not help sticking in his memory since he often watched the same feature three times straight during the noon-to-six matinée. He made sure he and his younger sister, Devorah, whom he always took along, were at the theatre an hour early to listen to the records that preceeded the screenings – waltzes, tangoes, the *William Tell* Overture, and an aria from Bizet's *The Pearl*

2 *Dybbuk*   1947
water-colour and ink
26.7 × 36.8 cm

Fishers. He remembered them all, though it was only much later he learned from his older brother who the composers were.

Moreover, the movie house was the first art school Iskowitz attended and the only one he enjoyed. For someone so fascinated by his own ability to capture likenesses, the faces flickering across the screen were not just those of actors and actresses but of models in a life class. 'I like expressive faces,' is Iskowitz's explanation of his early obsession with film. 'Say there was a big nose – that was great. The best thing I did was Bette Davis. Greta Garbo didn't turn out well, I don't know why.' Through films he made contact with movement presented in artistic form – moving pictures. They were his bridge to a community outside the impoverished, tension-filled ghetto. Life in Kielce did not make sense, but movies did.

It was not long after he began painting posters that Iskowitz's talent impressed the owner of the second movie house in Kielce. This man, who knew Iskowitz's father, arrived at the house one day to ask whether Gershon would make him some posters too. More confident now, he struck a harder bargain. He asked for a small cash payment per poster – enough to support an entire family for two days. 'So he gave it to me,' recalls Iskowitz, 'and I gave it to my father. Only I took some money to buy ice cream because it was summer – and, of course, water-colours, inks, brushes and paper.'

By the time he was nine or ten and earning his first money for his posters, Iskowitz had identified himself as an artist who worked hard, educated himself, and never asked anyone for a hand-out. Had there been a dozen movie theatres in the town he might have become a one-man poster industry; but the only other theatre was run by the Fascists and patronized by the Polish military. It was one more reminder that the Jews in Kielce were outsiders. The extent to which they lived their own life within the Leviathan of Poland is remarkable. They had their own social services, libraries, summer camps, schools, and newspapers. They operated a charity system to relieve the lot of beggars. In Kielce, Iskowitz remembers, Jewish landlords would not evict their tenants for failure to pay rent; and those with money to spare gave hand-outs to the poor. The majority of young people led highly organized lives revolving around the political parties they joined, which ran the gamut from Zionism to right-wing orthodoxy.

Iskowitz, never a joiner, did not sign up with any party; politics did not interest him. Still, he made use of party facilities whenever he liked and led an organized existence of his own making. He absorbed the many riches of the life he saw around him. He was particularly drawn to the local characters in Kielce, people who maintained their humour against all odds. There was the tailor who would stick his knee into the stomach of a pair of pants to convince a Polish farmer they would fit. And Moishe the carriage driver whose horse, an old nag purchased from the post office, insisted on stopping at every mail box on the way to the train station. 'The passenger missed the train so he took the carriage back home and the driver made double money,' he recalls. He befriended the water-carrier and the boy who sold bagels on the street. Like the people he admired the most he enjoyed a good joke. His brothers and sister loved chocolate but could not indulge their appetite for sweets very often on account of the price. However, the Suchard Company ran a contest in which anyone who collected all the letters MILKA WELMA BITRA printed individually inside the wrapping of small chocolate bars could win a three-pound bar. The letter B was so hard to get that nobody had won this giant treat for two years. Iskowitz got the right inks, turned an R into a B, and sent one of his brothers off to the shop to claim his prize. He performed this operation once every three months so the shopkeeper would not become suspicious. 'It was the only fraud I ever committed in my life,' he jests. In a more serious vein, Iskowitz says of his youth in Kielce before the war, 'It was a very real life, very real. What people told you

in those days, they meant. In our day and age, people tell you something one day and the next day, they change. In that society they were very honest with themselves: they tried to survive.'

The Iskowitz family appears to have made an art of survival. Gershon's namesake, Rabbi Gershon of Chęciny, a village fourteen kilometres south of Kielce, was thought to have performed a miracle and saved his hometown from destruction by fire. His grandfather, who was also born in Chęciny, was even more resourceful. He would lease fruit trees from Polish farmers in the area on a seasonal basis, paying a certain amount per tree, in exchange for which he could harvest the crop and sell it to buyers from the market. When the trees began to bloom in spring he would move into the orchard, where he slept in a little shack and kept a large dog to guard the precious fruit from thieves. In July he picked early cherries and, later on, wine cherries of a deeper colour. In the late autumn, keeping warm by building a small fire as evening fell, he harvested apples, pears, plums, and, finally, winter apples. 'My grandfather bought blind,' says Iskowitz, 'but he was a professional. He knew if a tree was healthy or not just by looking at it.'

Iskowitz's father, Shmiel Yankl, helped with the fruit-picking when he was a child. He always loved the country-side, but he had tasted city life, too. Around 1905, at the

9 *Water Carrier*   1952
gouache on board
29.8 × 39.4 cm

4 House on Leśna Street where Iskowitz lived and had his first studio

age of ten, he traveled 400 miles north by train to Warsaw, whose Jewish population numbered 350,000, equal to the entire Jewish population of pre-war France. He lived with his uncle, a man of means, who engaged a rabbi to teach him Yiddish for three months. He remained in Warsaw for about five years, reading Yiddish literature and anything he could find on the subject of medical science; but finding

Warsaw too large for his liking he eventually settled in Kielce. It was there, having grown a moustache to make himself look older, that he met and married a seventeen-year-old woman, Zisl Levy, whose father, Yosl, earned his living carving tombstones – 'a commercial artist,' Iskowitz calls him.

Shmiel Yankl and Zisl (the name means sweet) settled down in a rented section of a one-storey stone house on Leśna Street owned by one Kalmen Lazer and referred to as Kalmen Lazer's Hof. Another section of the house functioned as a *shtibl* or neighbourhood synagogue and study house where families attended services during the Jewish holidays. Shmiel Yankl, known simply as Yankl, ordered his furniture from his uncle, a cabinet-maker in Chęciny – shellacked chairs and beds and a large rectangular dining table. Electricity did not come to Kielce until the thirties so the house was lit by kerosene lamps. Butter was stored in a little cellar. The house was heated by coal, which was very expensive, and during the long Polish winters it was hard to keep from freezing.

Yankl made a modest living writing satirical pieces – poems, jokes, vignettes – for the weekly Yiddish-language papers in Warsaw, Radom, and Kielce; and continued his reading. Having become something of a healer through studying books on medicine, he bled neighbours suffering

3 Grandfather and two aunts

from colds by applying suction with cups. He always kept a bottle of 95 proof Polish vodka on hand for warding off germs. He was a *'folksman,'* says Iskowitz. 'He talked to everybody and loved to tell jokes. He always had friends.' Although he was oriented toward communism, his attitude was one of 'wait and see.' He did not take an active part in politics.

Yankl and Zisl had four children: Itchen (a form of Isaac), born in 1917, the year following their marriage; Yosl, named after Zisl's father, born in 1919; Gershon, born in 1921; and Devorah, born in 1925. Gershon was the wild child – nervous, temperamental, and disrespectful of authority. He would not answer any questions put to him by relatives or family friends unless they were phrased in a manner he considered appropriate. He was a fussy eater. He perspired a lot. A family photograph taken when he was around two, the year after he was kidnapped from his carriage by a woman who found him irresistible, could stand as an emblem of his situation. Yankl and Zisl look calm, even serene. Itchen and Yosl seem placid and well-behaved. Only Gershon stares into the camera with defiance. His eyes practically leap from the small square of paper.

At the age of four Iskowitz was sent to a nursery or kindergarten sponsored by the Lublin Yeshiva, one of the

5 Front row: Yosl, Gershon and Itchen
Back row: Zisl and Yankl

10 *Side Street* 1952
water-colour on board
50.8 × 61 cm

most highly regarded Jewish academies in Poland. His relatives fully expected he would become a rabbi and live up to the example of his namesake. However, Gershon thought differently. He 'had some papers' there and started to draw, although, he says, 'it really started when I was seven: I was more relaxed.' Relaxation was not possible at the school. The boys, who were all as young as Gershon, ate, slept, and studied together in big rooms. There was so much coughing and crying at night the emotional boy could not bear it. He needed space. A year-and-a-half later, by which time he had learned Hebrew and developed a lasting contempt for institutional life, he begged his father to take him out; his father agreed. 'I'm not an insider,' is how Iskowitz explains this episode in his life. 'I had to be outside all the time.'

For the next few months Gershon was tutored in Polish by a high-school student in Kielce who used to go out with his uncle; and when he turned seven his father registered him in the Polish public school as he had his other two sons. The principal, astonished that Gershon could speak Polish so well, wanted to put him in grade five but feared the twelve-year-olds would beat him up. Instead he was put into grade three – and was beaten up by the ten-year-olds. Iskowitz hated the Polish school even more than the kindergarten, though he did manage to learn German,

math, geography, and Polish history there. The principal, as it happened, was the secretary of the Polish Nazi party, the Narodowa Demokracja or Endeks, which organized pogroms all over Poland. Twice a week the eighteen Jewish children in Iskowitz's class were required to attend religious lessons taught by the principal's son, a Roman Catholic priest, who had only one sermon – the Jews killed Christ. That message was invariably translated into fights in the school-yard. Iskowitz had one more problem: the other pupils were jealous that he could draw better than they could. He lasted only two-and-a-half years at public school.

From 1930 on Iskowitz lived at home and did what he wanted to do – draw and paint. In the context of the Jewish ghetto, his freedom was a rare privilege. Most children, after studying the Bible at *cheder*, were apprenticed to a trade for five years, turning over any tips they made from errands and deliveries to their parents. Yankl did not apply this pressure to his children. As long as he could provide for them he let them do as they pleased. He took pride in outfitting his three sons before Passover every year in suits ordered from a tailor. 'Sometimes they fit, otherwise they were terrible,' Iskowitz recalls.

All the children drew. Itchen earned pocket money by doing architectural drawings for a Jewish architect. 'He

6 Zisl and niece

was a perfectionist, not as wild as I was,' says Iskowitz. Yosl drew once in a while and Devorah, who studied Hebrew at a girls' school, sketched. 'She was even better than I was,' Iskowitz allows. However, it was Gershon who took his talent to the extreme. By the age of seven, to everyone's amazement, he could draw a convincing likeness. He drew everyone in his family, his schoolfriends and the water-carrier. He even built himself a camera out of bits of wood and an eyeglass lens and took photographs of his mother and sister which he developed in Kalmen Lazer's basement workshop, with the help of a friend apprenticed to a street photographer.

Although his parents appreciated what he was doing, the other townsfolk did not. They were superstitious for the most part and drawing faces was taboo. Because he persisted in violating their fear, they called Iskowitz a bastard, a devil, a double personality. Even at seven he was isolated. 'When I started drawing at six or seven there were no galleries,' he says. 'I'd never seen a painting – only reproductions of paintings by a Polish artist named Kozak who specialized in horses. They made an impression on me but I wasn't influenced.'

The only people who could make him feel comfortable were his parents. 'The home was very unusual, very individual,' says Iskowitz. 'There were no fights, there was no interference.' It was Zisl who established the rhythm of the household. She had the baker's apprentice deliver fresh rolls to the house every morning; and every Tuesday and Friday she bought fresh cheeses and vegetables at the market. On Fridays she made a traditional stew called *cholent* which she took to the baker's to cook in his oven for the Sabbath. Every week, as times got harder, she cooked a big pot of pea or potato soup for the beggars who came knocking at the door. In the winter mornings, when it was too cold in the house for the children to get out of bed, it was Zisl who got up, made a fire, and boiled coffee or tea for them before they went on their way.

Both Zisl and Yankl were solicitous for Gershon's wellbeing. If either of them noticed he was sweating too much, they would march him out of the house for a walk in the park or a visit to the steambath; or sometimes Yankl would accompany him to a pine forest two kilometres away where he would sketch. During school vacations, he rented a cottage outside Kielce and, following family tradition, leased three or four trees for the summer from whose harvest Zisl made pear and cherry wine. Yankl, who knew Gershon loved music, did not neglect that side of his son's education. When Gershon was around eight Yankl took him on a visit to his brother's in Warsaw. A Polish production of the *Barber of Seville* was on at the time and Gershon

7 *Market* 1953–54
gouache on board
50.8 × 61 cm

wanted to see it. 'It was terrible – the singers were terrible,' he remembers, but Rossini has remained one of his favourite composers.

Best of all, Yankl partitioned off a room in the house so his son could draw in privacy; it was like the one he had made for himself, lit by one big lightbulb, in which to write. Iskowitz's first studio was near the south-facing window at the front of the house. Yankl set a wooden plank over the thick stone wall that protruded beneath the window and it was on this table that Gershon would draw his movie stars and, using the same German-made watercolours he buys today, paint the tree and sky reflections he saw through the window.

'The only thing that bothered me was that I wasn't doing what everybody else was doing,' Iskowitz recalls. 'I thought about it when I was very young. I used to play cops and robbers with the other kids and in the middle of a game I'd ask myself: 'What the hell am I doing here wasting my time'? So I went into my little room and started drawing. So you do your work – and then you get lonely. I couldn't figure out life when I was young. I had to take it and let it go – I had to accept myself. But I was worried how society would react to me.' Even at this stage in his life he had a fixed routine. He would draw for a half-hour or so, wander out into the street and meet some friends, stop in front of the music store to listen to Rossini and Verdi overtures piped through the outdoor speaker, and play a game of pingpong at one of the community centres or drop into one of the libraries affiliated with the three political parties. Knut Hamsun, the Norwegian writer of *Hunger* and *The Grey Man*, was his hero and 'the hero of every Jewish kid in my generation'; he was shocked to discover later that Hamsun was a Nazi. Having completed his circuit he would return to his room and draw some more. 'I was very restless,' he says. 'I was too far out in those days – not exactly abstract, but my work was very colourful.'

As the thirties unfolded it became more and more difficult to ignore the signs of impending disaster. In 1937 a savage pogrom erupted in Kielce and Gershon's older brother, Yosl, was struck on the head by a flying bottle. When Yankl and Zisl took him to the Polish police to demand justice, they were asked: 'Why the hell did you bring him here? He's still alive.' The Poles picketed Jewish stores with signs reading 'Don't buy from the Jews.' Anyone who dared leave the ghetto area after dark was terrorized. 'You knew something was going to happen,' says Iskowitz. 'It was too much. I was really scared, not for me but for my parents. We didn't know the Germans were going to come to Poland. The Jews only wanted a miracle to rid them of

the Poles. When the Germans came it was just a relief.'

Even so, people continued making plans for the future. In the summer of 1938 the Iskowitz family took their customary vacation in the countryside with Kalmen Lazer. In 1939 it appeared likely Iskowitz would enter the Warsaw Academy of Fine Art. His uncle had submitted some work on his behalf; and at the end of August 1939 he took the train to his uncle's to await the beginning of the school year. On September 1 the Nazis invaded Poland. Iskowitz returned to Kielce.

Following the orders of the High Command the Germans set the synagogue on fire and rounded up able-bodied Jews for enforced labour. Because they were on the look-out for anyone who wore a beard, the sure sign of being Jewish, all but the orthodox shaved. The Nazis, however, were not to be stopped by razors. They decreed that all Jews had to register their names with the Polish authorities. The ghetto area was bounded on either side by an iron foundry. One was called Henrikow, the other Ludwikow. The Nazis appropriated these factories for the manufacture of wagons for use by the German troops making their way to Stalingrad and Moscow through the mud. Iskowitz and his brother Yosl were both assigned to Ludwikow where they made wheel spokes. They worked during the day and at night returned to the ghetto.

8 *Burning Synagogue* 1953
gouache on board
48.3 × 35.6 cm

9 *Memory (Mother and Child)*   1951
water-colour and ink
50.8 × 24.3 cm

10 *Hunger*   1951
water-colour and ink
51 × 33 cm

11 Family and friends before the war

11 *Torah* 1951
gouache on board
43.2 × 53.3 cm

12 *Ghetto* 1947
water-colour and ink
35.6 × 48.3 cm

13 *Burning Town*   1952
gouache on board
30.5 × 40.6 cm

14 *Action* 1941
water-colour and ink
38.1 × 55.9 cm

In 1941 the Nazis sealed off the ghetto, so that anyone who wished to come and go needed a passport, and celebrated their deed with violence. Just around the corner from Lešna Street, in an alleyway that came to be known as Toite Gessele or Death Lane, German soldiers threw Jewish babies into the air and shot them. Iskowitz witnessed this act of random violence and recorded it in his earliest surviving pen-and-ink drawing, *Action*. The drawing shows a German solider with conspicuous teeth tearing a little girl from her mother's arms while running the fingers of his left hand through her hair. The mother's expression is anguished; her hands, as well as her daughter's, are wasting. The baby's hair has the texture of barbed wire.

The sealing of the ghetto did just what the Nazis wanted – killed off those Jews who could not withstand the typhus epidemics that broke out, or afford to pay the equivalent of $100 for a litre of milk on the black market serviced by the Polish peasants. 'Death by natural causes,' the Germans called it. By the time the ghetto was sealed it had absorbed Jews fleeing from Warsaw, Lodz, Cracow, and even Austria, who were in a position to buy food, but those with no money died on the streets. To make matters worse, the Germans posted signs promising ten pounds of sugar to any Pole delivering a Jew to the Gestapo, an offer many could not resist. The only privileged Jews were tailors and shoemakers, who were ordered to make clothes for the *Wehrmacht*. Whenever they could they brought back food for their families from the outside. To feed his family Yankl Iskowitz planted a small vegetable garden in a cave. Although the ghetto was patrolled by German guards, the garden was never discovered.

Worse was still to come. In September 1942 the Germans liquidated the Kielce ghetto. Every second day they took out three transports of Jews, each numbering 6000, leaving 1500 men between sixteen and forty behind for slave labour. Every deportee was permitted a twenty-pound parcel of belongings. Families were allowed forty-five minutes together before they had to assemble on the field. Yankl's message to his children was simple. 'Wherever you are, just take it easy,' he said, eliciting a vow from them that they should never take their own lives. The ghetto was liquidated in six days. A month later the Jews whose lives had been spared, at least for the moment, discovered the destination of the transports from a man who had somehow escaped: Treblinka. 'Everyone thought he was nuts,' says Iskowitz, who had watched the liquidation from the roof of one of the houses in the ghetto. 'I was looking down,' he says, 'and I started to draw. I drew it right on the spot.'

3 WAR YEARS

When the film based on Fanya Fenelon's book about an all-women's orchestra at Auschwitz, *Playing For Time*, was first screened on television in October 1980, critics touted it as a chillingly realistic portrayal of conditions in a Nazi concentration camp; Fenelon promoted her memoir to the status of a *cause célèbre* by publicly attacking the choice of Vanessa Redgrave, a noted PLO supporter, to play her autobiographical heroine. The niceties of the controversy were lost on Gershon Iskowitz. Not only did he refuse to watch the film but he considered its reception yet another illustration of his favourite Yiddish aphorism: *der oylem goylem* (The world is a dumbbell). 'If they showed it the way it really was,' he commented at the time, 'you wouldn't be able to watch it for a second.'

After Kielce was liquidated Iskowitz and his brother Yosl were transferred to the wheel factory at Henrikow and forced to live in crude barracks. Daily rations consisted of a piece of black bread and a bowl of soup. In the winter hunger was compounded by cold. Iskowitz tried to escape twice but both times he was brought back. He then began a series of barters which would extend over the next four years. He did a few drawings of Polish labourers, who were allotted larger food rations than the Jews, and of German soldiers, for which he might receive a loaf of bread or piece of butter.

One day in August or September 1943 (the only way to calculate dates by this time was to get hold of a discarded German newspaper and guess how many days had passed since it was printed) the Nazis rounded up 700 Jews and informed them they were to be resettled so their lives and work conditions would improve. They were herded onto a cattle-car bound for Birkenau, the annihilation centre of Auschwitz, the largest mass-killing installation built by the Nazis. The train doors opened to reveal a welcoming committee of ss men with whips and a swarm of Alsatian dogs. Immediately upon arrival the prisoners were subjected to a 'selection.' Those of no further use were directed to the right – that is, to immediate extermination; those still fit for work, to the left. They were stripped of their clothes and possessions, shaved of all their body hair, doused in chlorine, and marched through the camp, where they saw corpses strewn all over the road, bodies hanging from the barbed-wire fence, and a giant smoke cloud billowing in the sky.

Iskowitz was assigned to a two-storey barrack which held 600 people at Buno, a mile outside Auschwitz. A number had been tattooed on his left arm. He wore a thin jacket, a shirt, and a pair of pants, all made of woven straw, but no underwear or gloves. The jacket pockets were sewn up and inspected by a tailor every two days to ensure they remained that way. Prisoners were not permitted to warm their hands, even in the worst of the Polish winter.

Iskowitz's job was to haul hundred-kilo bags of cement to be used for extending buildings at the camp. Although precise dates had become meaningless, eliminating both the past and future tense, each day proceeded with numbing regularity. At four in the morning the prisoners were awakened by shrill whistles and marched outside for *Appell* or roll call, which might last two hours. Breakfast, which had to provide nourishment for a fourteen-hour workday, was a piece of black bread, a slice of cheese, and coffee substitute. The rest of the daily menu consisted only of thin cabbage soup. There was a place to wash – that is, if a prisoner had the energy to splash himself with rancid water outside and run back to the barracks to dry out: the Nazis did not provide towels. 'Nobody would believe it,' Iskowitz once remarked. 'You walked around like the living dead. You didn't know where you were. Your senses were taken away. The food was poisoned so everyone would die a slow death. The Nazis used prisoners for their labour and performed medical experiments on them. I was lucky.'

At 6:30 AM the prisoners filed through the gate to work. Over the gate stretched a sign that read: *Arbeit Macht Frei* – work makes you free. An orchestra posted at the gate played Strauss waltzes and symphonies to give this message some meaning. At 8 PM the returning work details passed under the gate again to the sound of music and stood outside for a second *Appell*, which might go on even longer than the first. 'There was absolutely no relaxation possible at Auschwitz,' one survivor has written in what now sounds like a humorous understatement. How could a prisoner relax when, in addition to the murderous daily routine, the random killings and omnipresent disease, the infamous Dr Mengeles would arrive every two weeks to conduct a 'selection,' pointing with his immaculate white gloves sometimes to the right, sometimes to the left? Thousands of prisoners who had lost the will to live and succumbed to shock – the passive suicides the Germans called *Muselmanner*, or *Moslems* – were dispensed with in this way.

Asked to describe his state of mind at Auschwitz, Iskowitz replied: 'You're just hungry and you just want to eat – nothing else. If your mental stability could still function, you survived. If not, forget about it.' Using whatever strength and intuition they could draw on, the prisoners adapted to the extremities imposed by a government which believed it had arrived at the Final Solution of the Jewish Question: systematic mass extermination of an entire people. At the cement factory Iskowitz pieced together a pair of mitts and a little cap from the tattered remains of

15 *Selection Auschwitz* 1947
water-colour and ink
40.6 × 50.8 cm

old trousers. He set aside empty cement bags made of thick paper and, when no one was looking, shoved them inside his striped jacket as insulation against the cold. In performing these seemingly small acts of resistance he was trading off the preservation of life against the chance of instant death: when the work teams returned to the barracks every night an ss guard armed with a club stood at the gate watching for suspicious bulges inside a jacket, listening for the telltale crunch of paper.

If death had become a random matter, so had the means of survival. The Jewish doctors at Auschwitz, for example, were granted special privileges, such as better and larger food rations (although they also could be killed instantly if the Nazis decided they knew too much about the operations of the camp). One Dr Silber, a physician from Paris, took a liking to Iskowitz and instructed his son to arrange a clandestine rendezvous. He offered Iskowitz some of his own soup, but it proved so much richer than the prisoners' cabbage soup that he came down with diarrhoea. However, Dr Silber's protective instincts sometimes met with greater success. He hid the nervous young man in his office several times so he would not have to parade, naked, before Dr Mengeles.

In the face of this absurdity and terror the last thing one might expect Iskowitz to do in Auschwitz would be to draw, but the contrary was true. He used anything he could get his hands on – bits of brown paper and German inks bribed from the guards, coffee substitute, stray pieces of cardboard. He even received a few commissions. One of the guards at the cement factory, 'bored with killing,' showed him some snapshots of his wife and children. Iskowitz asked for some paper and copied them on the spot. His reward: an entire loaf of bread and a salami. 'It was like getting a million dollars,' he says. Another time he was approached by a guard who asked: 'Herr Jude, what do you do'? 'I am a *Kunstler*, an artist,' he replied. 'You are a *Judenschwindler*,' said the guard, who nonetheless requested a line drawing of Der Führer. Again Iskowitz received payment in food.

Although he drew portraits to relieve his desperate need for nourishment, his art served a personal need. At night, when the other prisoners were asleep, he would sit on his bed drawing the madness he saw around him – images of death, dying, and hard labour. 'I did it for myself,' he remembers. 'I needed it for my sanity, to forget about my hunger. I needed it to calm down.' Iskowitz left hundreds of drawings under the floorboards in the barracks. He never dared show them to anyone because he knew the barracks were infiltrated by Nazi informers – 'they chose the thin ones,' he says – disguised as prisoners. He was not alone in attempting to set down a record of life in Auschwitz. As Janet Blatter and Dr Sybil Milton note in their

16 *Moon: Buchenwald* 1952
oil on board
25.4 × 34.3 cm

Art of the Holocaust, over 30,000 works of art by concentration camp prisoners survived the war buried in crocks, behind stones, or in niches, sometimes wrapped around the legs of smugglers who got them out.

In late 1944, winter having closed in again, the prisoners at Auschwitz were transferred west to Buchenwald, a camp located eight kilometres from Weimar, Goethe's birthplace. The Russian army was advancing steadily westward and, as time ran out, the Nazis were desperately trying to complete their annihilation programme and cover their tracks. The prisoners were forced to make the 257-kilometre journey to Buchenwald on foot and by train. It took eight days. Individual rations for the move consisted of half a can of horsemeat and a loaf of bread. Many died of fatigue and starvation along the way. On arrival they found that Buchenwald was more tense even than Auschwitz. Bullets were scarce so it became imperative for the Nazis to think of other ways to commit murder. They took groups of prisoners on long death marches, driving them through the fields until the weak and sick and old fell dead to the ground.

Iskowitz played sick on arrival at Buchenwald. After so many years in the camps he had come to understand the German mentality. Why should the Nazis waste a bullet on someone who was obviously about to die from 'natural

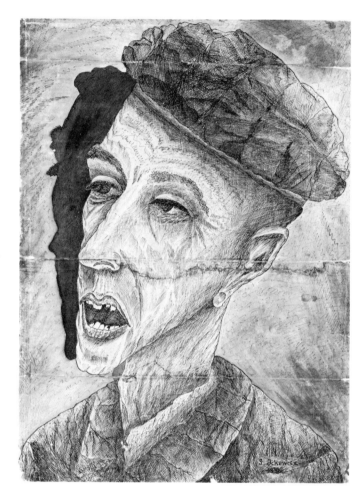

17 *Condemned* 1945
water-colour and ink
68.6 × 50.8 cm

12 *Buchenwald* 1944–45
water-colour and ink
38.1 × 50.8 cm

18 *Escape* 1948
oil on canvas laid on corrugated paper
36.8 × 45.7 cm

causes'? His sole purpose was to conserve whatever energy he had left by moving his body as little as possible. He did permit himself one exertion. Whenever the guards asked for volunteers to go by train to Weimar and clean up the rubble left in the wake of Allied bombings, Iskowitz raised his hand. For one thing, there was the likelihood of finding bread or salami in a shop; and, for another, who knew what could be salvaged from the debris? One day he struck it rich. Among the ruins of a bombed art-supply store he discovered little sheets of paper and cakes of water-colour paint. He stitched the cakes into the pockets of his uniform and upon his return to the Buchenwald infirmary dissolved them in ersatz coffee – and drew. He painted a large head of a man which he later called *Condemned*. The yellowish face is long and sunken, covered with lines like a scroll. An inky shadow along its right side sets it into relief so the eye of the viewer cannot escape what it sees. It is a portrait of absolute exhaustion. The man's mouth is open but his eyes are dead.

At the beginning of April 1945 rumours began circulating among the prisoners at Buchenwald that the Nazis were about to dynamite the camp to destroy all traces of their activities. In one final act of self-preservation Iskowitz attempted to escape. He was shot by a machine gun in the left knee and, falling from the barbed-wire fence, broke his hip. The guards left him for dead but friends in the camp brought him back and cared for his wounds. Two weeks later, on April 11, 1945, the American army entered Buchenwald. There was no doubting the date; time could once again make sense.

Iskowitz weighed eighty pounds when he was liberated. In addition to his leg wounds, he had suffered heart and lung damage. However, the war years had changed him in more drastic ways. He had lost his parents, his brother, Itchen, and his sister, Devorah, at Treblinka; his brother Yosl disappeared one day at Auschwitz. In losing his family he lost his past. Three million of Poland's 3.1 million Jews had died. There were no Jewish communities in eastern Europe anymore, no synagogues, no *cheders*, no water-carriers and bagel-hawkers. And yet he had learned a valuable lesson through the bitter schooling he received in the war. He had discovered inside himself a tremendous will to live, a love of life, which was inseparable from his need to keep drawing and painting. It is his experiences at Auschwitz and Buchenwald that allow him to say, now, that 'If you have got talent, you have got everything. It's all in yourself: you discover yourself.' At the age of twenty-three Iskowitz left Buchenwald with two drawings and a head full of memories. His experiences had aged him but in many ways, as he himself realized, 'I was just a kid.'

4 MUNICH

19 Iskowitz and painting of poet I.L. Peretz, 1946

After the liberation Iskowitz was removed to a hospital for prisoners near Buchenwald and then, because doctors suspected he had tuberculosis, to a sanatorium in Blankenhain, east Germany. Both hospitals were administered by the occupation army. He began a slow and difficult recovery, gaining five or six pounds every week even though his stomach kept rebelling against a proper diet. Unable to walk because of his leg wound, he was confined to bed. 'I couldn't move but I could still draw,' he later recalled. Using whatever came to hand – newspapers, sheets of stationery – he retraced the faces he had become familiar with as a boy in Kielce: Charlie Chaplin, Laurel and Hardy, and the Yiddish writers I.L. Peretz and Sholem Aleichem.

When it was ascertained Iskowitz was not suffering from tuberculosis, he was transferred to a hospital in Feldafing, a town thirty-five kilometres south of Munich near the Italian Alps, where he continued to mend slowly. It was nine months before he could walk again. Meanwhile, a few of his friends from Kielce who were living in a displaced persons' camp near the hospital came to visit him. Early in 1946, after he was discharged from hospital, Iskowitz joined them at the camp, sharing their huge room in a villa near the Stamberger See. If concentration camps were hell, camps for displaced persons were limbo. The main busi-ness of the day was waiting – waiting for refugee organizations to locate relatives abroad, waiting to hear which of one's family and friends were alive and which had died, waiting until a visa came through and you were allowed to leave for another city and start again. Meanwhile you could at least console yourself that things could only get better.

Iskowitz's luck manifested itself in strange ways. At the end of the war a few of his former acquaintances from Kielce decided to return to the town to have a look around. Before they left he told them about the two drawings he had hidden in an attic the day the Germans began to liquidate the ghetto. When the men returned to the DP camp they presented him with one of the drawings – *Action* – which, although eaten away by moths, was still where Iskowitz had left it. The return of the drawing was a tiny miracle that illuminated an otherwise confused time. 'It was tough,' Iskowitz has commented on his years in Feldafing. 'I didn't know what to do with myself. I didn't know anything about galleries or exhibitions. I just drew every day.'

At the end of 1946 he was accepted at the Munich Academy after submitting his drawings and going for a test. This was his first and last experience of formal study and he quickly grew to hate it. 'Every day was like a night-

20 *Waiting* 1947
water-colour and ink on board
41.9 × 54.6 cm

mare,' he once commented, but since he was trapped in Germany for the time being and searching for ways to develop as an artist, he stuck it out as long as he could. Every day he took the train from Feldafing to an old castle in Munich where the academy, whose building had been destroyed during the bombing of the nearby concentration camp, Dachau, had been relocated. Everything about the academy revolted him, from the strictly enforced rules to the German students who, he says, were still anti-Semitic. He did, however, get his paper free. All art supplies other than these rationed materials had to be obtained on the black market, and Iskowitz availed himself of this source too. Every two months he received a food parcel from the Joint Distribution Committee, an American organization which provided relief to refugees – tinned corned beef, packages of Chicago salami which had dried to hard blocks during the ocean voyage to Germany, a carton of cigarettes, and a package of coffee. He sold the cigarettes and coffee on the black market and with the money bought paints.

Even as a boy Iskowitz had loathed institutional life, and his contempt for authority increased a thousand times in the concentration camps. He quickly made an enemy of one instructor at the academy, a descendant of the great German romantic painter, Caspar David Friedrich. Fried-

21 *Action*   1948
oil on canvas laid on board
40.6 × 58.4 cm

22 *Through Life* 1947
water-colour and ink on board
54.6 × 32.3 cm

rich, Junior, was a man in his seventies and went by the rules. Every day he assigned Iskowitz a still life. Overwhelmed by boredom, Iskowitz began to sneak into the life class in the room opposite, despite his fear of being found out. It took a few weeks before Friedrich noticed his absence and hauled him off to the principal. Tears in his eyes, Friedrich protested he had given the rebel the finest subjects in the world – pears, apples, oranges, and a bottle. Iskowitz responded: 'I like to eat them, not to paint them.' He was expelled for his insolence, then reinstated, a routine repeated more than once before he finally left the academy for good a year-and-a-half later.

It was at the Munich Academy, however, that he met the important expressionist painter, Oscar Kokoschka, who came once a week to inspect the students' work. Kokoschka was the first known artist Iskowitz ever met. He had not even heard of Picasso, Matisse, or Braque at this time; nor did he know who Kokoschka was. However, Kokoschka was so impressed by the young man's drawings that he asked to see more, and even rode out to Feldafing to look at his Buchenwald drawings. He talked to Iskowitz about form and composition and, most important of all, encouraged him to keep working.

During the summer vacations Iskowitz had a part-time job painting sets for the Munich Opera, temporarily housed at the Printzregenten Theatre. In payment he received special ration cards for restaurant meals and enough money to buy paints. He painted sets on cheap linens for productions of *Il Trovatore*, *Aida*, *La Bohème*, *Don Carlos*, *Lucia di Lammermoor* – but the commission that excited him the most was the set design for the first act of the *Barber of Seville*, the opera he had seen performed in Warsaw. The manager showed him photographs of the original set, which had been destroyed along with all the others – a street running through Seville. Iskowitz had his own ideas, which did not conform to the photographs. Instead of painting one street, he 'opened up the city' by adding a side street. He used brighter colours than his instructions called for. The Munich critics were not impressed and accused Iskowitz of tampering with the traditional image of the opera. He was fired.

From then on he continued his education on his own. For the first time in his life he started to go to art galleries. He saw group shows of the work of Kokoschka and another noted German expressionist, Max Liebermann, in small galleries in Munich, and once he stumbled across paintings by Monet and Bonnard. They struck a chord. 'I'd never seen art before in my life,' Iskowitz recalls. 'I really liked it. I didn't understand it, but I saw the space and also the consideration of light.'

At the DP camp he began a series of water-colours depicting his past in which he continued his own exploration of light. He built them up layer upon layer of bright translucent washes over a base of Chinese white, drawing in the figures with black ink. In these extraordinary works he began to transform his memories of suffering and violence into images of beauty, patterning his colours symbolically – red for death, white for innocence. He painted a selection at Auschwitz, marbling the sky and the uniform of the ss guard pointing to the left in scarlet. The group of naked prisoners, much smaller than the guard and receding into the distance, radiate light. Two of the water-colours show the interior of the barracks, where the prisoners, each one a little Gershon, are lying on their bunks near a small violet table. There is no dirt or squalor or evidence of misery; these have all been absorbed into a desire to commemorate the human spirit. The most anguished painting is *Yzkor*, dominated by a single bloody candle with its flame still lit. On either side of it black figures melt into pools of red. One tiny figure stands at the base of the candle with arms outstretched. His small gesture of hope, although almost invisible, represents the human drama of history striving to make itself felt against the vast backdrop of eternity. The theme of *Yzkor* runs through all the remaining water-colours of the series, which took Iskowitz years to complete.

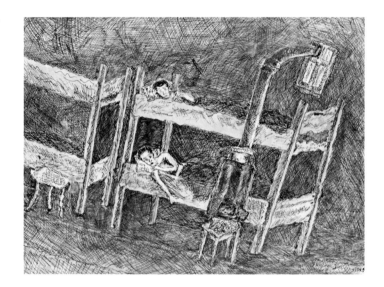

23 *Barracks*   1947
water-colour and ink
38.1 × 50.8 cm

24 *Yzkor* 1949
gouache on board
30.5 × 40.6 cm

There is one oil portrait in this series, of Iskowitz's mother, Zisl. It is a tender picture but one need only compare it with the self-portrait he did the same year to see how much more difficult it was for him to paint his mother than himself. The self-portrait is a facial landscape with bold contours wrapped around a garden of roughly-applied colour. Zisl's portrait is almost static by comparison. The background of the painting and her dress merge in an unbroken mass of soft green. The most haunting aspect of the face is the eyes – transparent blue spheres that bespeak endless serenity.

In 1947 some of Iskowitz's work was exhibited in group shows, the first of which took place in Munich. A while later someone (he cannot remember who) arranged a show in Paris of his concentration camp scenes, including the two he did in Buchenwald. Since he was not permitted to leave the DP camp legally, he stole out through Strasbourg to attend the opening. Smugglers were posted at the border in Germany and France and, for a price, they arranged the train and the passage across the border. In Paris he stayed with a relative for three weeks but did not feel up to exploring the galleries. After the opening of his exhibition someone told him Picasso and Braque had both been there. This could not have meant much to him at the time: he had still not discovered Picasso.

Toward the end of the year he was smuggled out of Feldafing again, this time to go to Italy. He had a friend in Modena from his time in Buchenwald who kept his promise to contact him after the war. Iskowitz spent four or five months painting in Bari, in southern Italy, and enjoyed himself immensely. The paintings he did there went on view in a gallery in Modena. The dealer gave him a suitcase of lire for his work but since the lire was next to worthless, it was more a gesture of appreciation than anything else.

The trips to France and Italy were pleasant diversions but Iskowitz's main concern at the time was arranging his visa to Canada. While he was in Paris he wrote to the Jewish Congress in Toronto stating who he was and who he was looking for – mostly relatives from his mother's side of the family brought over to Canada by his granduncle, Chaiml, who left Kielce in 1909 to seek a more prosperous life. The officials succeeded in tracing his relatives and they set about organizing his application. This was not as simple as might appear. Canada had a quota system for Jewish refugees, although if a displaced person had a brother or sister already in the country there was no problem. In the case of uncles and aunts things took longer. Iskowitz's Uncle Benny, his mother's twin brought over by Chaiml in 1911, put down some money but had to

25 *The Artist's Mother* 1947
oil on canvas laid on board
50.8 × 40.6 cm

13 *Self Portrait* 1947
oil on canvas laid on board
50.8 × 40.6 cm

insure Iskowitz would not become a welfare case. It was left to Gershon to work out the details. He went to the Canadian consulate in Munich and began by having a general check-up. Although his health had improved considerably, he walked with a permanent limp. The consul rejected his application because of his leg. 'I'm an artist,' he protested, 'my leg has nothing to do with it.' But the consul's word was final.

'Always, when my life was in danger,' Iskowitz found, 'I did a drawing and I pulled through.' This time was no exception. Iskowitz had met a Miss Shapiro who worked for the Joint Distribution Committee, whose European headquarters were in the same building as the Canadian consulate. Immediately after Iskowitz's disappointing interview she walked out into the hallway and asked what had happened. Hearing he had been rejected, she told him to bring in his paintings. She took them into the consul and arranged a second interview. This time the consul was drunk. Through a German interpreter he rambled on and on, until finally Iskowitz interrupted him by turning to the translator and saying in German: 'Give me a paper and pen and tell him to sit still.' A few moments later he had completed a big line drawing which he presented to the consul as a gift. The stunned man stood up shakily and grasped Iskowitz's hand. 'You're going to be a famous person in Canada,' he said. 'There will be special privileges for you on the boat.' Iskowitz replied tactfully: 'I don't want to be famous. I want to be good.'

The boat was a military transport with a thousand passengers, mostly Croatians. The trip over took ten days, during which time Iskowitz slept in the engine room. His special privileges consisted of playing pingpong with the captain and drinking scotch. For the most part he spent the time worrying whether he would be able to make out on his own. 'My father used to give me money for paper and water-colours. I wondered myself what was going to happen to me.'

Iskowitz landed in Halifax in September 1949 and from there he took the train to Montreal, where he stayed with a friend for a day. The sight of 'so much empty land' impressed him, but the train finally arrived at Toronto's Union Station. His family was there to meet him: Uncle Benny; Frieda, the widow of his mother's oldest brother, Yankl; Hilda, his mother's youngest sister; and from his father's side, his grandfather's second wife who had come to Toronto with her two daughters after her husband died, some twenty-five years before. They were complete strangers to him. 'My cousins in Poland were much closer,' he remarked later. 'These were all strange people – I'd never met them before.' Once again he was the outsider.

5 TORONTO

'When I came here, there was nothing. I knew nothing. I hated it.' Iskowitz gave this description of his arrival in Toronto still wincing with the pain of it, thirty years after his train pulled into Union Station. He was certainly grateful to have finally left Germany, but the experiences of the previous ten years had done nothing to calm his nerves. Everything about Toronto, including the hot, humid, September weather, irritated him. He spoke no English. Adrift in an unknown landscape he struggled desperately to connect with life as he remembered it before the war.

He went to live with his Aunt Frieda and her son, Bobby, in their house on Rusholme Road in the west end. He lasted two weeks with his relatives, long enough for them to persuade him to introduce himself to Canadians as George, and for his Aunt Frieda to caution him as she pointed at a drunk lying in the gutter across the street: 'Look, Gershon, that man is an artist.' As the Levys saw it, anything was preferable to becoming an artist, even selling nylons or buttons. At least they were steady jobs and an ambitious person could make something of them. Iskowitz disagreed. His Uncle Benny offered to send him to university but he refused, preferring odd part-time jobs in warehouses along Spadina to enrolling in another academy. Clutching a few of his drawings he went for a job interview at a Christmas light factory on Dupont Street, where Frieda's sister worked as a secretary, but the owner rejected him because he did not think he should be wasting his talent on lightbulbs. Iskowitz missed his father, who used to support him as well as reassure him whenever he became frightened by his own strangeness.

He had so little money at first that finding adequate living space was difficult. He tried one boarding-house after another in the predominantly Jewish neighbourhood where his aunt and his uncle lived but the strict house rules always drove him out. Women visitors and private telephones were not permitted. The food consisted of too much potato and too little of anything else. Worst of all, the Jewish landladies who ruled over their establishments with such zeal had nothing better to do than gossip about the boarder with no visible means of support who spent the nights painting, and wondering aloud whether he could possibly pay his rent. 'I didn't want people to get to know me,' was his attitude. 'As soon as they became suspicious about what I was doing, I moved.' Before finding his own studio in 1962, he had tried a dozen different lodgings.

The art scene in Toronto, or whatever little of it was visible, disappointed him too. At the Roberts Gallery he came upon paintings by the Group of Seven, which struck him as German expressionism two or three times removed.

14 *Apple Orchard*   1952
oil on canvas laid on board
40.6 × 50.8 cm

15 *Yzkor* 1952
water-colour and ink
30.5 × 40.6 cm

He made the rounds of the Laing Galleries, Douglas Duncan's Picture Loan Society, and the Hart House Gallery, and found he had exhausted his list. At the Art Gallery of Toronto, as it was then called, he discovered the featured exhibitions were group shows organized by art societies such as the Ontario Society of Artists and the Royal Canadian Academy. Although he was not yet familiar with the names of Picasso and Chagall, he knew at once he was in a provincial backwater; and he could only console himself by thinking others were in the same position as himself.

He first hesitated to show anyone his concentration camp drawings or talk about the war because he did not want people to feel sorry for him. His arrival in Toronto was noticed by a few students at the Ontario College of Art, however, who had heard he was an expressionist like Arshile Gorky and expected him to commit suicide at any moment. 'I'm not an expressionist,' he told them. 'I'm a painter.' From time to time a few of the students at the college drove him into the countryside around Uxbridge, Markham, and Muskoka on sketching trips; sometimes he took the bus and sketched on his own. One of the students told him about the twice-weekly life classes – or sessions, as there was no instructor – at the Artists' Workshop, situated in a little church at the corner of Sherbourne and Bloor streets. Since they cost only fifty cents an hour he became a regular there from 1951.

26 *It Burns* 1952
gouache on board
50.8 × 66 cm

16 *Miriam* 1952
gouache on board
38.1 × 26.7 cm

Mainly, though, he kept to himself. Uppermost in his mind was completing the series of water-colour memories he had begun in Munich. He had brought eleven with him, and in two years after 1950 he painted another twelve. Fire is their predominant motif – scarlet flames burning across deep violet skies. He painted the rabbi of Kielce removing the scrolls from the burning synagogue, contorted bodies heaped in a pile in the town square, men and women with packs on their backs being driven to their fiery destiny, a blood-stained moon rising over the huts in Buchenwald. The space in which the flattened figures seem suspended gives the water-colours a child-like quality which only heightens the feeling of powerlessness he wished to convey. His experience as a scenery painter shows through, too, in the way he organized the paintings to look like luminous stage-sets against which his tiny heroes and heroines act out their assigned roles.

There is one exceptional portrait in this series, of a girl named Miriam who had lived next door to the Iskowitz family in Kielce. Miriam was three or four years younger than Iskowitz, closer in age to his sister, Devorah. She would have been about fifteen when she was killed in the war but Iskowitz painted her as she might have looked in 1952 had she survived. Miriam's hair clings to the deep purple background like a thick blue vice. Her face is violet

27 *Barrier*   1952
gouache on board
50.8 × 61 cm

28 *The Wall*   1952
water-colour and ink
59.7 × 45.7 cm

and pink, her eyes black coals, her expression one of intense unstoppable pain. The most startling thing about her, however, is her open blood-red mouth, the mouth of all the women and men he drew during the war. It is also the portrait of Devorah, the dark-haired sister he loved so much.

While these paintings filled a personal need they did not pay the rent. Small portrait commissions helped, although even they did not always turn out as expected. Through contacts in the Jewish community he was asked to do a portrait of a family of four. He painted them one by one, joining them together as he went along. However, the mother of the house was upset that the picture was not in the style of photographic realism she was expecting and ordered her husband to return it, which he did with many apologies and a small cheque. When Iskowitz received his next commission, a portrait of an elderly woman's Siamese cat, he painted it over the previous one. By chance, the first woman's husband met Iskowitz on the street years later and asked for the return of the painting; Iskowitz said he would look for it and walked away.

In 1953 he was hired to teach art classes one evening a week at the Holy Blossom Temple, the reform synagogue on Bathurst Street. His students were mainly Jewish businessmen but there was also a dentist who boasted he

29 *Explosion* 1952
gouache on board
50.8 × 63.5 cm

30

32

31

33

30 *Untitled*   1952
felt pen
21.1 × 27.9 cm

31 *Untitled*   1952
felt pen
21.1 × 27.9 cm

32 *Untitled*   1952
felt pen
21.1 × 27.9 cm

33 *Untitled*   1952
felt pen
21.1 × 27.9 cm

34

had once fixed Winston Churchill's teeth. Depending on how many people showed up with their two dollars, Iskowitz earned between $10 and $20 a week. He taught still-life painting but one night his students requested a life class. The next week Iskowitz brought along Georgette Culot, a model who used to pose at the Artists' Workshop; but Georgette in the nude was more than the businessmen could cope with. Amused by their embarrassment as they watched her strip, Iskowitz turned to the model and said: 'Georgette, please put your clothes back on – this is a holy place.'

Gradually his horizons were beginning to expand. He started dropping by Avrom Isaacs' framing shop on Hayter Street where he met Isaacs' assistant, Tom Gibson, a painter who worked as a set designer at the CBC. In the evenings he went drinking at the Embassy Tavern and met photographer Michel Lambeth, who visited him in his room on Borden Street and took his picture. He met Michael Snow and Graham Coughtry.

In 1953 he heard of a group show that was to hang at Malloney's, a combined bar and exhibition space on Grenville Street. Paintings by OCA professor Eric Freifeld, Ernie Taylor, an illustrator for the *Toronto Telegram* who painted ships of the Great Lakes, and Taylor's friend William Coryell, a graduate of OCA, were included. Just as Taylor

35

34 *Untitled* 1952
felt pen
27.9 × 21.1 cm

35 *Untitled* 1952
felt pen
21.1 × 27.9 cm

36 Iskowitz, Borden Street

and Coryell were hanging their pictures Iskowitz came down the hall with some of his Munich paintings under his arm. 'His eyes are full of eagerness and hope and he's got a bad limp,' Coryell remembers saying to Taylor. Although Taylor did not know what to make of the paintings, Coryell liked them – 'they were primitive and a little rough,' he says – and invited Iskowitz to hang them. A generous, eccentric man who now paints scenery at the CBC, Coryell proceeded to take Iskowitz under his wing. 'He needed somebody,' he remarked. Coryell visited him regularly in his room where the two men listened to *tziguener-reizen* on Iskowitz's record player and drank sweet Hungarian wine.

Iskowitz would always complain to Coryell about the lack of places to exhibit, although that was beginning to change. In 1954 the first exhibition of Painters Eleven was held at the Roberts Gallery. The paintings of this loosely-organized group, which included Jack Bush, William Ronald, and Harold Town, caused a sensation. It brought into focus some of the energy of Toronto painters eager to break through to the mainstream of modern art. Iskowitz followed this development with curiosity and interest but could not identify with the sources many of the group drew on – cubism and expressionism. That same year he showed two of his concentration camp drawings at the annual exhibition of the Canadian Society of Graphic Art at the Art Gallery of Toronto, but that did not satisfy him either. 'Everybody was shocked,' he recalled. 'Nobody could figure me out. There were rules in those days. Drawings didn't count as graphics if they were in colour. They put me into a category: Gershon Iskowitz does personal things. If you didn't belong to a group or society or academy, you weren't an artist.'

It was Coryell who finally engineered Iskowitz's escape from the frustrations he was experiencing in Toronto. One day in 1954 he decided to take 'George,' as he knew Iskowitz, up north to 'Bert's place.' Until 1958 Bert Weir ran a summer school for painting and sculpture at McKellar, 24 kilometres north of Parry Sound. Weir and his wife, Elena, had both graduated from the Ontario College of Art. They would invite their friends from the art school to stay at the lodge at McKellar, located on a picturesque site between two lakes. In exchange for room and board and whatever they made from teaching, these artist-friends gave lessons to people who rented cabins on the property; and they had the chance to exhibit their work at the lodge. 'George always wanted a place to show his paintings,' Coryell said, 'and Bert showed them.'

As Coryell expected, Weir and Iskowitz quickly became friends. 'Bert's a great person for opening people up and

37 *Eric Freifeld*   1955
oil on board
50.8 × 38.1 cm

getting them to paint,' is how he explains it. The warm environment was just what Iskowitz needed and before long he related to the Weirs as his surrogate family. Bert and Elena had two daughters, Sky and Wave (Reed was to follow), of whom Iskowitz became very fond. Bert's mother, who did all the cooking, used to bring him tea in the afternoons while he sketched and painted. 'He was very shy and polite; he didn't talk much at first,' recalls Elena; Bert remembers him as a 'gentleman' who always shaved in the morning. Weir's school was by no means overrun with students or artists, but there were always a few on hand to compare notes with. Tom Gibson visited, as did Gerald Scott and Bob Cowan, a painter from New York who had studied under Hans Hofmann. 'It was beneficial for everyone,' says Weir. 'We lived as a unit, talking all the time. It was a beautiful time. Gershon usually sat back in a corner and listened. Then he would throw up his hands when he couldn't stand it anymore and go back to his painting.' In this friendly, relaxed atmosphere Iskowitz flourished. 'When he first came,' Weir remembers, 'we had the impression he could hardly put his brush to the page on account of his nervousness. As he returned year after year, you could see him quietening down. He needed the retreat from the city – a place where he could always be sure of enough food and a place to sleep.'

38 *Landscape*   1954
oil on board
29.7 × 35.1 cm

39 *Landscape* 1954
oil on Masonite
27.9 × 36.5 cm

40 *Parry Sound* 1954
oil on board
40.6 × 50.8 cm

From 1954 to 1957 Iskowitz was a regular guest at McKellar, one year spending six months with the Weirs and often visiting during the winter, too. It was at McKellar that he began to get 'closer to nature and people.' He became a student of the Ontario landscape, learning its movement and colour and rhythms. 'That man painted all the time,' says Weir – seven or eight sketches every day, and drawings and paintings at night. He painted nature directly and emotionally, on pieces of Masonite and the backs of Weir's discarded canvases. His painting *Midnight* (1955) is one of the best of the McKellar group. He painted it from the studio window, very quickly, using bold black and white strokes to define a large tree to the left and concentric yellow and orange rings to convey the tortured beauty of the moon rising over the lake. The deep blue background is flayed by streaks of light, as the images threaten to burst their black outlines. *Midnight* is charged with the excitement Iskowitz felt at discovering a new world.

During his summers at McKellar, and on winter days, too, when he painted the winter light with socks on his hands, a hole punched through for his thumb, Iskowitz continued investigating the relationship of colour to the landscape. When it was warm, he lay on the grass staring upward through the trees, or sat on a huge rock above the lake, looking down at the shapes below. He promised himself that one day he would go farther north and look down from a greater height.

Whenever he returned to Toronto he discovered some new gallery had opened and within days he was through the door with a few paintings in tow. In 1955 Avrom Isaacs opened the Greenwich Gallery (which became the Isaacs Gallery in 1959) and in the summer of 1957 he hung a few landscapes from 'Bert's place' in a group show with Michael Snow and Graham Coughtry. The same year he was in a group show at the Hayter Gallery, the first co-operative exhibition space in Toronto. It was a good year for galleries, though most of them had short lives. Toronto critic Paul Duval and two partners opened the Park Gallery on Avenue Road, and on Gerrard Street Barry Kernerman inaugurated the Gallery of Contemporary Art backed by the Hirshhorn family. Iskowitz promptly turned up at Kernerman's gallery and introduced himself to Dorothy Cameron, an excitable Jungian overflowing with boisterous laughter and good cheer, who was working there until she had gained enough experience to open a place of her own. What he remembers of Cameron is her smile; she, in turn, was struck by his limp and his shyness. 'You could imagine him in a concentration camp,' she said, although by that time Iskowitz had been living in Toronto for almost

41 *Midnight*   1955
oil on board
60.5 × 69.7 cm

42 *Parry Sound No 1* 1955
water-colour
22.9 × 30.5 cm

43 *Parry Sound No 2* 1955
water-colour
22.9 × 30.5 cm

44 *Parry Sound No 3*   1955
water-colour
22.9 × 30.5 cm

45 *Parry Sound No 4*   1955
water-colour
22.9 × 30.5 cm

46 *Swirling Night*   1955
oil on canvas laid on board
20.3 × 25.4 cm

47 *Autumn Skies*   1955
oil on canvas laid on board
25.4 × 35.6 cm

ten years. 'He was very drawn, very shy. He hobbled in from Hayter Street where he had hung a few things. He had a dark, dreamy, passionate face. He brought in that first pile of water-colours – the burning town, people running. I was just knocked out by them.'

Kernerman did not give Iskowitz a show: his gallery closed at the end of 1958 when the Hirshhorns withdrew their support. However, the same year Dorothy Cameron opened her gallery, the Here & Now, on Cumberland Street, where she represented such artists as Florence Vale, Toni Onley, Louis de Niverville, and Maxwell Bates. It was there, on February 26, 1960, that Iskowitz had his first one-man show in Toronto. 'I have gone out on the limb for a young Polish painter because I feel that his talent is enormous and unusual,' Cameron told *Globe and Mail* reporter Mary Jukes. The exhibition consisted of one concentration camp drawing, one Munich painting, and a number of layered water-colours of the landscape around McKellar that he had done from memory in 1959, the year he could afford his first canvas. In these paintings he had begun to refine inessential details from his work, concentrating instead on creating a mood through the use of colour. He painted boldly streaked skies, sunsets, and clouds in shades of orange, yellow, and blue. 'The extraordinary thing about it,' said Cameron in 1980, 'was that by

48 *Dusk* 1955
oil on board
27.3 × 21.6 cm

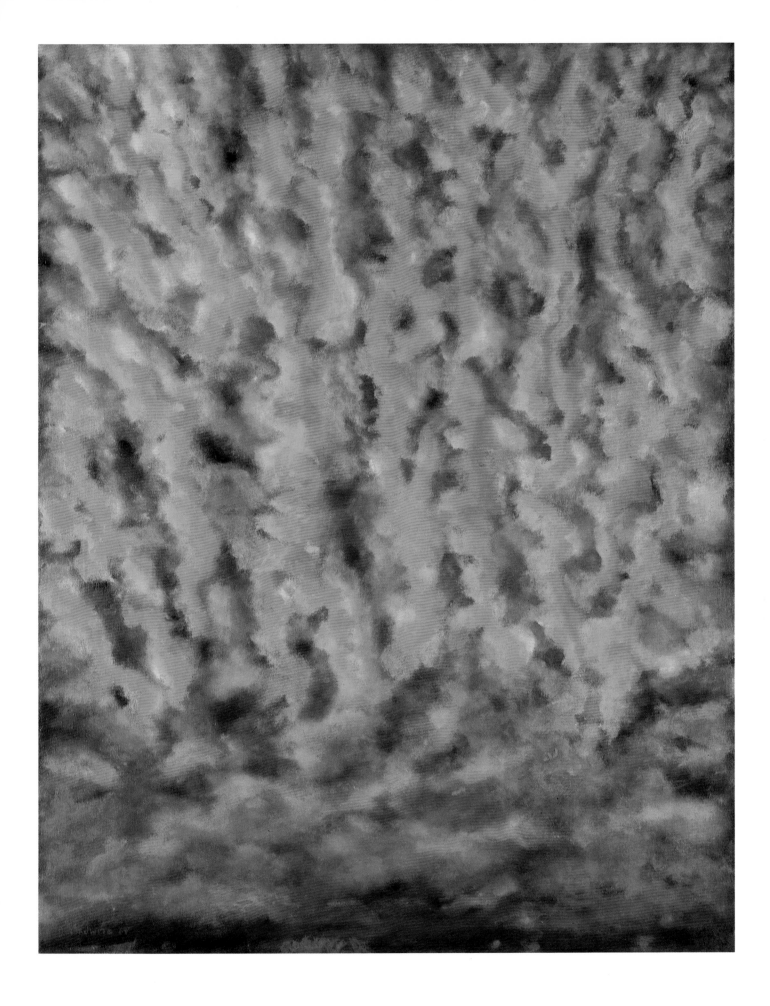

the time he had his first show, there was a joy and serenity in everything he was doing. He'd taken the Canadian landscape and just turned it into something *we* never saw in our own landscape. He saw this lovely, soft, romantic golden afternoon and blue tender sky.'

The exhibition was reviewed in all the papers. Robert Fulford referred to 'the gentle poetry' of the paintings in the *Toronto Star* of March 5. 'Each picture is a sonnet in paint – a poet-painter's love poem to the spacious freedom of Canada's land, water-ways and skies,' wrote Colin Sabiston one week later in the *Globe and Mail*. Only Elizabeth Kilbourn, writing in the *Hamilton Spectator*, noticed a dark side. 'He has painted the Canadian land-scape in a way it has seldom been seen before. Out of waves of colour which at once convey physical depth and mental agony, the forms of trees and rocks and hills erupt with dramatic inevitability. This is earth and sky painted with an intense, personal and disturbing vision.' The ex-hibition was a turning-point for Iskowitz. 'At first he was a thing apart,' Cameron remarked. 'He was a shy observer. He always went to everybody's shows and people from the beginning had respect for what he was doing. When he had his first show, people who had seen him in the back-ground were really so generous. They were glad to see he really could paint. Because he wanted to be an artist so much, they were always afraid it was just a dream of his.'

49 Iskowitz in Spadina Avenue studio, 1981

17 *Sunset* 1960
oil on canvas
127 × 101.6 cm

18 *Autumn Reflections* 1962
oil on canvas
125.4 × 100 cm

19 *Sunset* 1962
water-colour
24 × 33.5 cm

During the twenty years Iskowitz lived and painted in his studio on Spadina it remained unchanged, as though exemplifying Walter Moos's dictum: 'Outside signs of success are wasted on Gershon – he doesn't need anything except paint.' In 1972 Peter Mellen described it in six pithy sentences: 'A long room with a skylight. One end partitioned off for sleeping. Canvases carefully stacked against the wall. Paint tubes neatly laid out in long rows. Everything in its place. Nothing superfluous.' That description was true in 1962 and it held until the end of 1981, though Mellen might have included an inventory of the furnishings: a lumpy divan, four hassocks splitting at the seams, a small fridge permanently stocked with vodka, a rectangular coffee-table holding a mother-of-pearl shell ashtray, a cluster of family photographs pinned to one wall. A bare enumeration of contents, however, does not explain why Iskowitz became so identified with his studio that he was considered as much a fixture on Spadina Avenue as the warehouses, factories, wholesale outlets, restaurants, and bars lining the wide thoroughfare. The significance of his move to Spadina lies in one extraordinary fact: it was the first time in his life he lived alone. In Poland he had lived with his family and in concentration camp barracks; in Germany, with friends in a DP camp; in Toronto, in a series of boarding-houses none of which had

a separate entrance. Now, on Spadina and College, at the age of forty-one, he had privacy at last. The next ten years would prove endlessly fertile and productive.

As soon as he moved into his studio his pent-up emotions overflowed into a river of paint and ink. He worked as a man driven, beginning with a series of pointillist pen-and-ink drawings of the Ontario landscape. Seen up close they are just masses of black pinpoints and twitchy little hooks but at a distance they arrange themselves into the shapes of trees, streams, reflections, and mists of rain. Then, using the ideas he got from the drawings, he began work on a canvas larger than any he could have considered installing in his cramped quarters on Borden Street. He was searching for a sense of space and an image of life which would express everything he had learned about the Canadian landscape – and himself – since he first began studying its lineaments in 1951. That image turned out to be a transparent tree whose leaves and branches appear to be emerging like an enigma through a mysterious shroud of atmosphere. The painting, *Spring*, is a romantic celebration of both solitude and unity with nature. It is a strong autobiographical statement as well as a description of the landscape; and it prefigures an entire body of work in which recognizable images begin to disintegrate, float, and move in a disembodied dance to the strains of ethereal

50 *Spring* 1962
felt pen
12.5 × 50.2 cm

20 *Spring* 1962
oil on canvas
165.4 × 140 cm

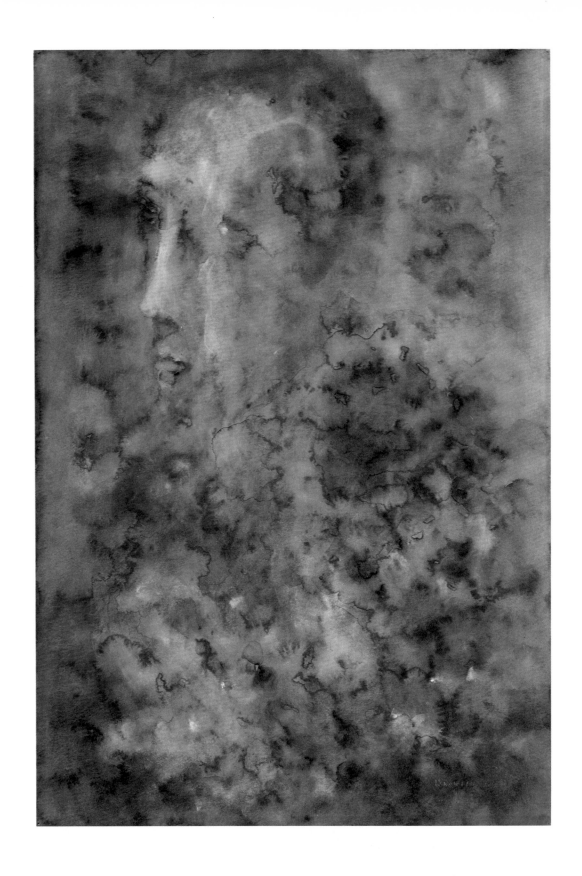

21 *Self Portrait*   1963
water-colour
71.1 × 50.8 cm

22 *Seated Figure*   1964
oil on canvas
68.6 × 58.4 cm

music. 'From the fifties my work was influenced by Vivaldi – that's very important,' Iskowitz has said. 'The first time I heard it, it got me.'

After completing *Spring* Iskowitz began a series of water-colours in which centred female figures simultaneously vanish and emerge into the landscape. The women are featureless and almost formless, their arms and legs melting into the layers of gouache that hold them in a dark embrace. Iskowitz did not continue to pursue these figments in his coming work, though he has continued drawing women's portraits for his own pleasure. 'What was I going to do – the same seated figure over and over?' he once offered by way of explanation. 'If I have to repeat myself I'd get bored to death. Besides, the figure is still there in the forms, in the landscape.'

The pointillist drawings, the canvases *Spring, Summer,* and *Autumn,* and the figurative water-colours form a single cadence whose closing bars were marked by another important change in Iskowitz's personal map. Dorothy Cameron, who had relocated her gallery, renamed the Dorothy Cameron Gallery, on Yonge Street, had fallen on hard times. She was spending too much money and knew it was only a matter of months before she would be forced to close. She managed to keep the gallery going to 1965 but some time in the preceding year, knowing how sensitive

Iskowitz is to disruption and dislocation, she took steps to place him with another dealer, Walter Moos, an ironic gentleman with an inordinate capacity for detachment and doing business. She could not have made a more astute choice.

Moos is a born dealer. His uncle and aunt founded Galerie Moos in Karlsruhe, Germany, in 1899, and were joined by his father, Friedrich; a few years later his uncle opened a branch of the gallery in Geneva. Moos's past bears a certain resemblance to Iskowitz's. Although he did not go through the camps, his family did. When Moos, born in 1926, was thirteen, the Germans deported his family to Marseilles. His parents were killed and he was placed in a children's home. In 1942 he escaped to Switzerland and earned a diploma at the Ecole Supérieure de Commerce. After the war he moved to New York and studied economics and advertising at the New School for Social Research, eventually working as assistant to the export manager for New American Library. In April 1959 he left that position to open Gallery Moos in Toronto and join in the struggle to bring Toronto into the mainstream of contemporary art. 'Gershon came to Canada on the eve of day one,' he once remarked. 'I came on day one.'

In Moos, Iskowitz found the ideal dealer, an alter ego who is as fiercely loyal, secretive, and imbued with

51 *Untitled drawing* 1958
felt pen
56 × 42.8 cm

23 *Untitled* 1964
oil on canvas
50.8 × 76.2 cm

24 *Autumn Images* 1965
oil on canvas
76.2 × 61 cm

25 *Autumn Sky* 1964
water-colour
71.1 × 88.9 cm

26 *Parry Sound Variations* 1965
water-colour
58.4 × 45.7 cm

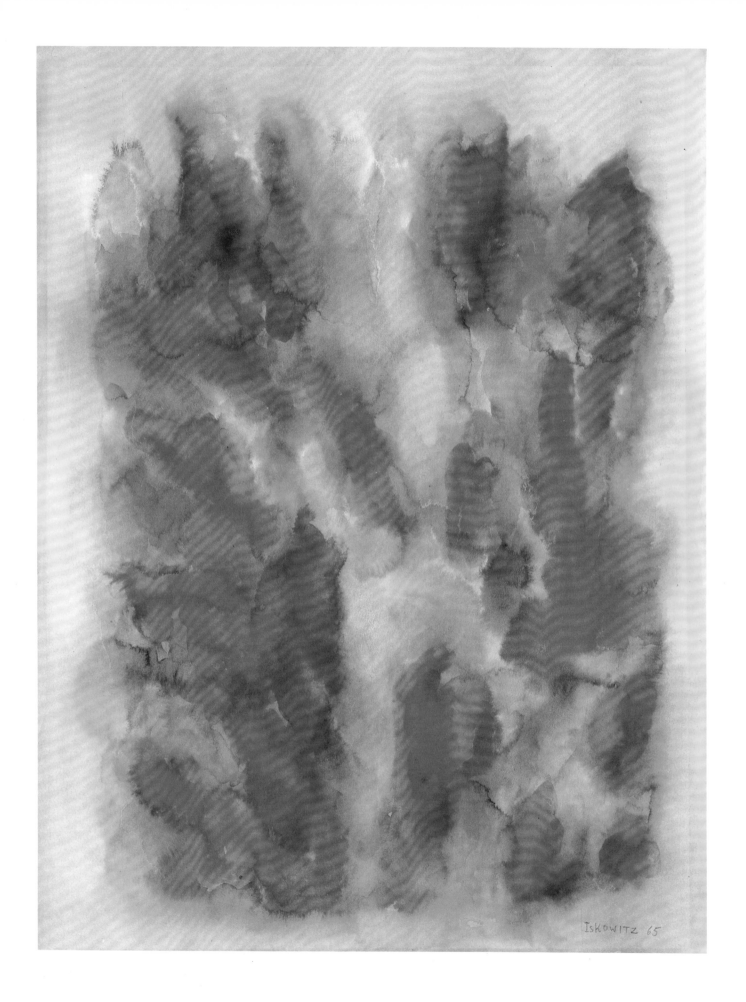

27 *Parry Sound* 1965
water-colour
66 × 78.1 cm

28 *Sextet* 1965
oil on canvas
152.5 × 122 cm

29 *Summer Sounds*   1965
oil on canvas
172.7 × 139.7 cm

European attitudes and traditions as he himself. From 1964, when he first exhibited with Moos, Iskowitz has relied on him absolutely to protect his privacy and represent him to the sorts of people he has never sought to communicate with through any other channel than his art. He will not take a single step in exhibiting or publishing his work without first consulting Moos, invariably replying to all enquiries with the two little words: 'Ask Walter.'

The security provided by Moos is reflected in Iskowitz's paintings of 1965, which mark the beginning of a new period or cadence in the gradual evolution of his thought. Sensing he 'needed to loosen up, to find more space,' he painted only four or five oils that year, channeling most of his energy into a series of thirty water-colours, the Parry Sound Variations. In these he dematerialized the landscape even further, by setting his images of nature free from the hold of the horizon and dispersing them across the paper in delicate waves of colour. A painting such as *Summer Sounds*, one of the best of the Parry Sound Variations, is, like every successive painting, a summation of everything that came before. Its rays of coloured light refer back to the flames of *Burning Town*, the rippling movement of *Midnight*, the streaked sky of *Sunset*, the luminous branches of *Spring*. The figure of a woman is there too; it is felt like a strange presence hovering behind the paint. The

accomplishment of 1965 is still a source of satisfaction to the artist. 'I like that period,' he says. 'It got me right through.'

From 1966, when the Parry Sound Variations were first shown, scarcely a review appeared in which Iskowitz's painting was not described as lyrical, joyous, or happy. Every article began with an obligatory capsule biography to explain the miracle of his transcendence. It is as though Canadians could not bear to think of an unhappy Iskowitz. It never occurred to critics to consider why a man would image his situation in the portrait of a single wind-swept tree, or spend so much of his time thinking about skies.

By the mid-sixties the Toronto art scene was undergoing a period of transformation and expansion; or as Walter Moos might have commented: day two had finally dawned. For the first time in Toronto's history, art and glamour coincided and artists became the subject of intense public interest. Harold Town, Robert Markle, and Graham Coughtry wrote newspaper articles about their travels, opinions, and eating habits. Fashionable people made a point of being seen at exhibition openings. Cameras flashed, sales increased, and the Eatons threw large parties for Toronto's art set. It was no longer possible for professors at the Ontario College of Art to hold up the Isaacs Gallery for ridicule.

30 *Summer Blues* 1966
oil on canvas
81.3 × 101.6 cm

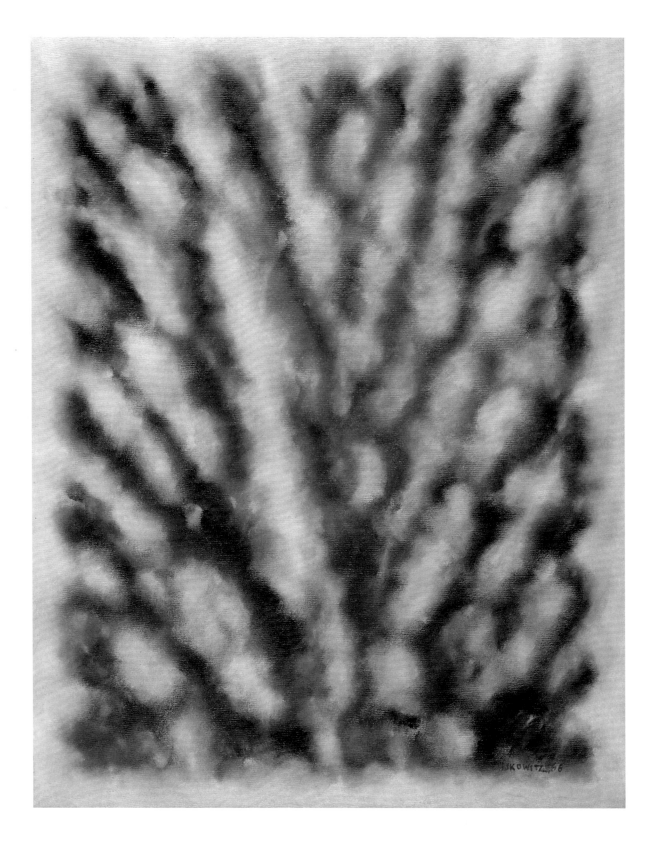

31 *Summer Skies* 1966
oil on canvas
102 × 82 cm

Iskowitz was not part of the 'in' crowd but he shared in the excitement by becoming a willing guru to a group of artists in their twenties, fresh out of art school and anxious to connect with whatever was going on. He could not have avoided this role even if he had wanted to. The four blocks between College and Dundas bounded on the west by Spadina had become the focus of the art scene. For a while it seemed everyone lived on Spadina – Coughtry, Gordon Rayner, Robert Hedrick – and if you did not live there you came there to drink at Grossman's or the Victory Burlesque, to buy art supplies at Gwartzman's, or play jazz at Rayner's studio. By 1965 moving to Spadina had become almost mandatory for young artists: David Bolduc, John MacGregor, Karl Beveridge, Carol Conde, Dan Solomon, and Jerry Santbergen all had studios there. Iskowitz found it easier to relate to these artists than to his contemporaries; and they, in turn, found him more accessible than the artists who had become media darlings. 'He was not self-important or always puffing himself up,' said David Bolduc. 'He was a very gracious guy.'

He expressed that graciousness in a variety of ways. Although, as Carol Conde has remarked, 'it was almost a privilege if you got to go into his place,' he occasionally cooked borscht and hamburgers for a group of friends over at her place. Usually he held court at night at Grossman's

Tavern where he freely dispensed lessons in lifestyle and professionalism, or offered comments about work-in-progress, his own and that of other artists. He was held in great respect by his young entourage. 'Iskowitz was not about stardom,' Conde elaborated. 'There were people on Spadina with greater ladder mobility but you didn't associate with Gershon for that. He had high morality. He would give three Canada Council recommendations a year and if you were deemed one of the three, that was a high privilege. He epitomized what we all had gone to the Ontario College of Art to find. The dream you had of the art world, he was in reality. All those fairytales about the art world – Rembrandt and the Sistine Chapel – there's someone who *was* that fairytale.'

Iskowitz never betrayed the advice he handed down at Grossman's Tavern, always preferring to stay at home and work out a new idea to searching for inspiration in New York, Spain, or India, which had become the favoured destinations for many Toronto artists. In 1966, still cresting on the energy of the Parry Sound Variations, he began his Spring, Summer, and Autumn Landscape series, which took him through 1967 to complete. He does not paint the winter, he once joked to a reporter, because it is too cold. For the first time he made a distinct division between the foregrounds and backgrounds of his paintings, eliminating the horizon completely. In the Summer Landscapes of 1966 he generalized the intensity and warmth of that season to the point where each canvas bore six jagged blue stripes, radiating upwards from a fixed point at the bottom of the canvas which symbolized the horizon. Speckles of gold, orange, and green peek out at the edges of the stripes, suggesting the flickering of the sun through leaves and branches and creating an aura around the shapes which gives the illusion of distance between them and the mottled grey backgrounds.

The following year, as he continued the Landscape series, he broke up the stripes into oval-shaped patches of colour streaming evenly across the canvas, each surrounded by flecks of coloured light playing around the edges. In the summer landscapes the patches are turquoise and dark green; in the spring landscapes, pale yellow or grey-brown; in the autumn landscapes, orange, mauve, deep blue. Although they reminded one critic of multiplying cells, Iskowitz considers them leaf shapes. 'In 1966, when I painted the summer, spring, and autumn,' he explained, 'I was painting the landscape looking up through the trees; but in 1967 everything was falling down. The leaves were *falling down.*'

With the leaf shapes of 1967 Iskowitz had fully explored the perspective of standing on the ground and looking up or straight ahead, which he had first adopted in the fifties in the Markham area and McKellar. As he boldly puts it, 'I did the ground.' Now it was time to leave earth behind and rise over the landscape. Ever since 1958 he had been thinking of going to the far north, but in 1967 a casual incident jogged his memory. At a dinner party one night he was asked whether his paintings, which seemed to shimmer like the northern lights, had in fact been inspired by a trip to the Arctic. They had not. That innocent question set him thinking: was there a landscape out there that corresponded to his interior map? 'I went to find out if I'd been right. I wanted to find out how things were happening *down*. You've got to paint from every angle, to find something new. Some artists and scientists predict space but they don't experience it personally.' He received a Canada Council travel grant for $1750 and in September hired an RCMP helicopter to fly him from Winnipeg to Churchill. 'I couldn't believe it,' he said. 'I was shocked.' Diving over Churchill he discovered more space and brighter colours than he had ever imagined – enough space for him to feel completely at home. He saw bright colours exploding through layers of cloud, land masses breaking through atmospheric barriers, dramas enacted on epic scale by the protagonists – space, form, and colour. The experience overwhelmed him. He stayed in Churchill for three or four

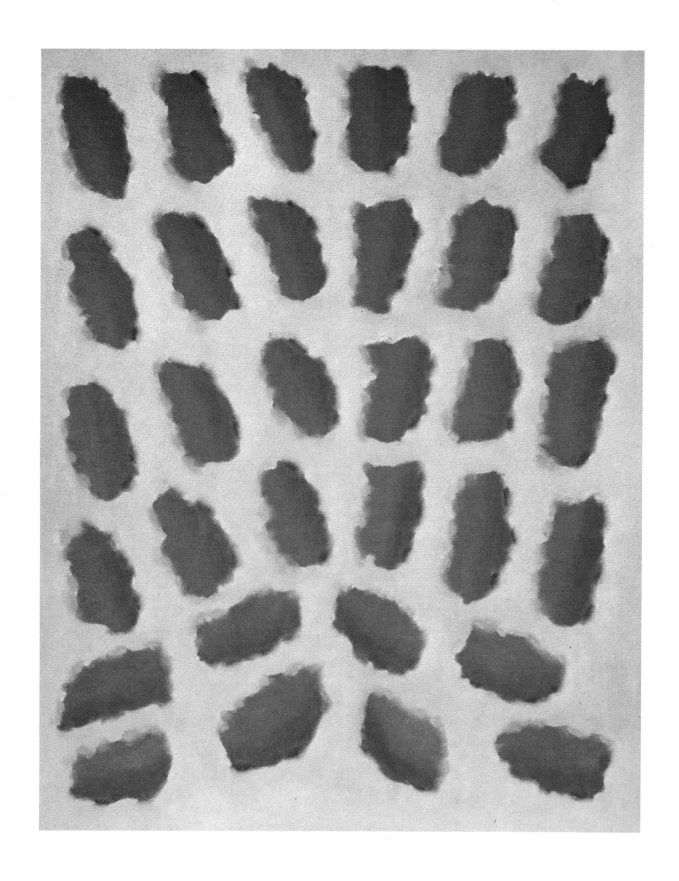

32 *Autumn Landscape No 6* 1967
oil on canvas
152.4 × 122 cm

33 *Autumn Landscape No 5* 1967
oil on canvas
152.4 × 127 cm

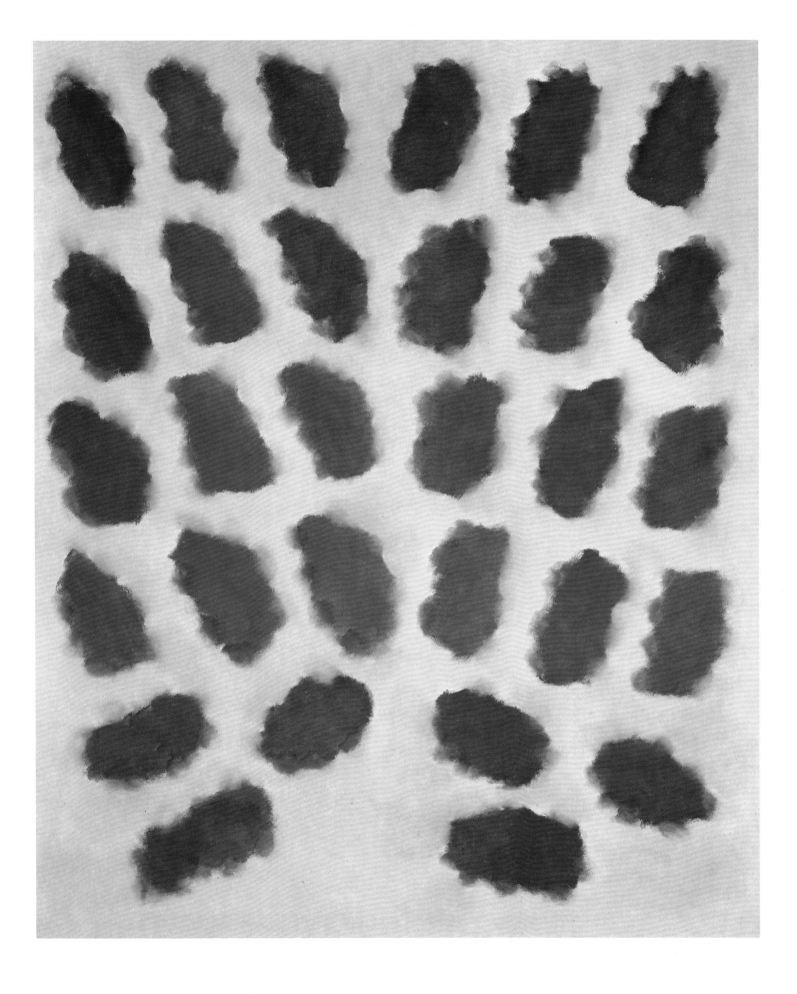

days, flying over the landscape by day and returning to his hotel room in the evenings to sketch. The night before he returned to Toronto he invited his pilot, a man in his twenties, to have a look at the sketches. 'I see these things all the time,' said the pilot excitedly. Iskowitz accepted the remark as the highest compliment.

On his return to Toronto Iskowitz increased the size of his canvases in keeping with the scope of his magnified vision; he broadened his concept of design and his colours became bolder, brighter, and even more lucid than in the early and mid-sixties. The turquoises, violets, flame reds, and supersonic greens he had used in his 1952 watercolours of Kielce re-emerged in these enormous portraits of *down*. It is tempting to see them as the surprising but logical resolution of a movement begun in 1942, when he stood on a rooftop in the ghetto drawing the violence below. His own explanation is more succinct: 'The colour came through experience and a much freer approach to composition. Looking down is different – there are lots of huge spaces.'

The first paintings he did after his trip to Churchill were *Seasons I* and *Seasons II*, dedicated to Vivaldi, and which he refers to as the 'the northern lights.' Significantly, they are both diptychs, the first time he had attempted them. 'Diptychs are a challenge – I can take any painting of mine,

34 *Seasons No I* 1968–69
oil on canvas
254 × 355.6 cm (diptych)

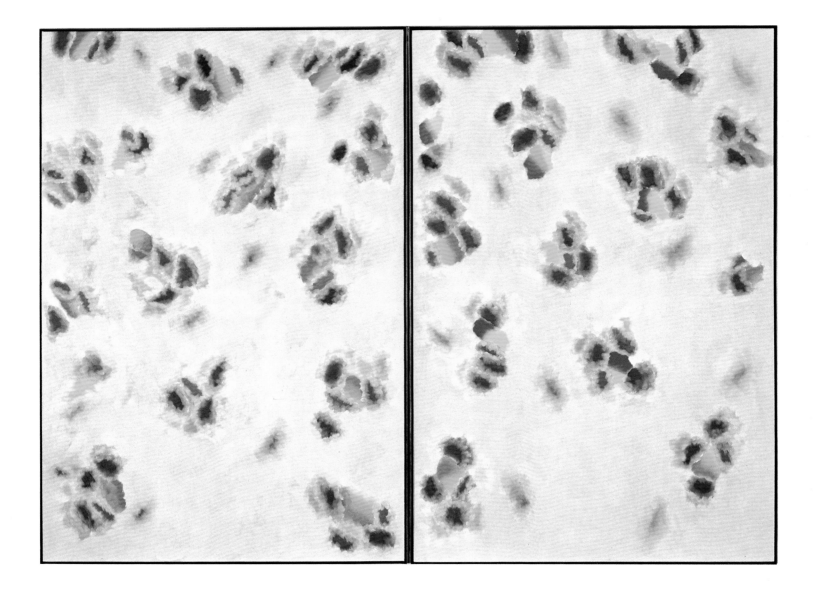

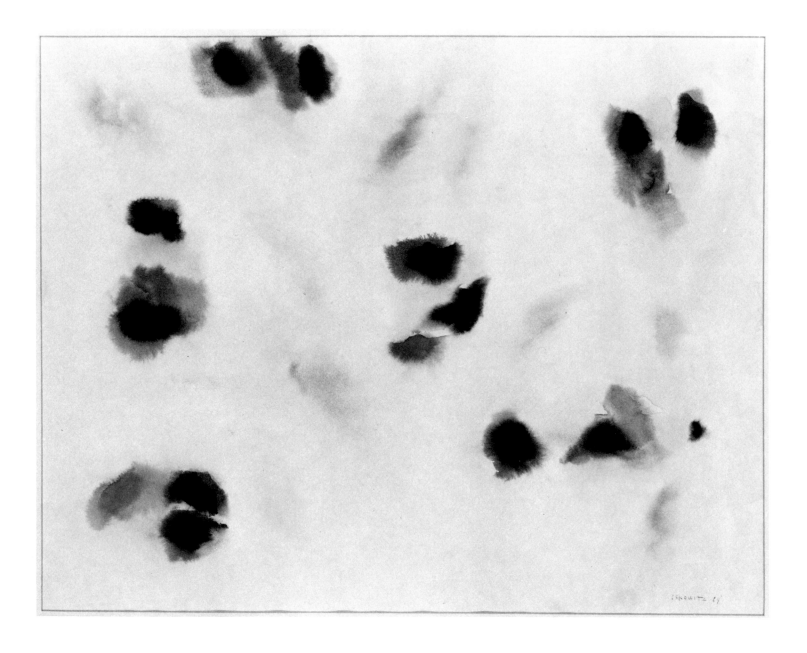

35 *Lowlands No 13*   1970
oil on canvas
152.4 × 121.9 cm

52 *Western Sphere No 11*   1969
water-colour
47 × 62 cm

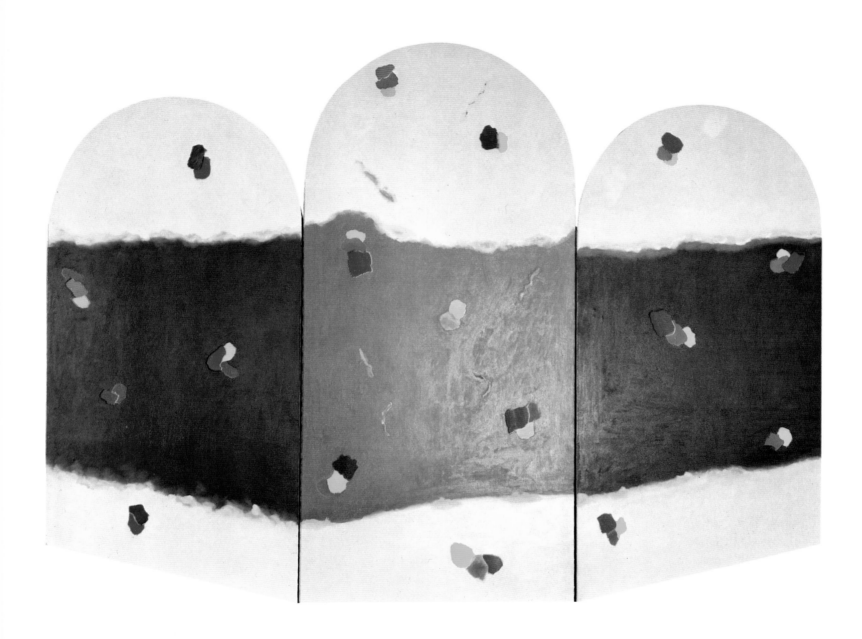

36 *Triptych* 1969–70
oil on canvas
274.3 × 139.7; 304.8 × 152.4; 274.3 × 139.7 cm

even a water-colour, place it beside an oil, and the two will form a unity, they will make sense. Other artists' diptychs look like fights. Mine are a unity.' In *Seasons I* and *II* clustered knots of colour tear through pale pink skies. The size of the paintings (254 × 356 cm) gives them grandeur; and the interplay between the colour clusters and the softly layered fabric of the backgrounds carries them into a temporal dimension. The colours appear to glow, then disappear, then reappear in a different place, re-enacting the drama of memory as it lights on one image, then another.

The most spiritual painting to come out of Iskowitz's first experience in the far north, however, is the enormous triptych, *Triptych*, which only became feasible economically in 1969, two years after his return. This is the only time Iskowitz has employed a shaped canvas; and he used the money he received from the sale of *Seasons* I to the National Gallery to defray the expense of its construction. The three panels are dome-shaped. The middle panel is the largest (304.8 × 152.4 cm), with a level base; the two smaller end panels (274.3 × 139.7 cm) slant upwards at the bottom. The two sets of allusions, the first to cathedral windows, the second to a helicopter windshield, work in counterpoint, evoking both introspection and a view of the world outside. A thick continuous band of intense colour – deep blue on the outer panels, aquamarine on the middle

one – floats across the whole, punctured by Iskowitz's personal calligraphy: brightly coloured dots and shreds of colour which flicker through the blues and the surrounding pearl-grey ground. *Triptych* is an environmental work which engulfs the viewer without suffocating him, providing limitless space for meditation.

In September 1971 Iskowitz flew north again, this time to James Bay, and returned to Toronto with a new set of impressions. Immediately he began experimenting with different colours and colour massings – red, purple, green, orange, blue – to express the contours and mysteries of the northern landscape. Those paintings, which convey what he saw and felt as the helicopter climbed high, he called Uplands; those which crystallize his sensations as the helicopter swept down through the clouds, Lowlands. His flights north had not changed him, only refined his ideas and given him new energy. He became a connoisseur of space and an intimate of light.

Breaking through to his masterful vision of *down* was a personal triumph which led to still another personal triumph. In 1972 the National Gallery selected Iskowitz and sculptor Walter Redinger to represent Canada at the Venice Biennale. For Iskowitz it was a dream come true, a sign that his long voyage from a Polish *shtetl* through the darkness of Auschwitz and Buchenwald had been

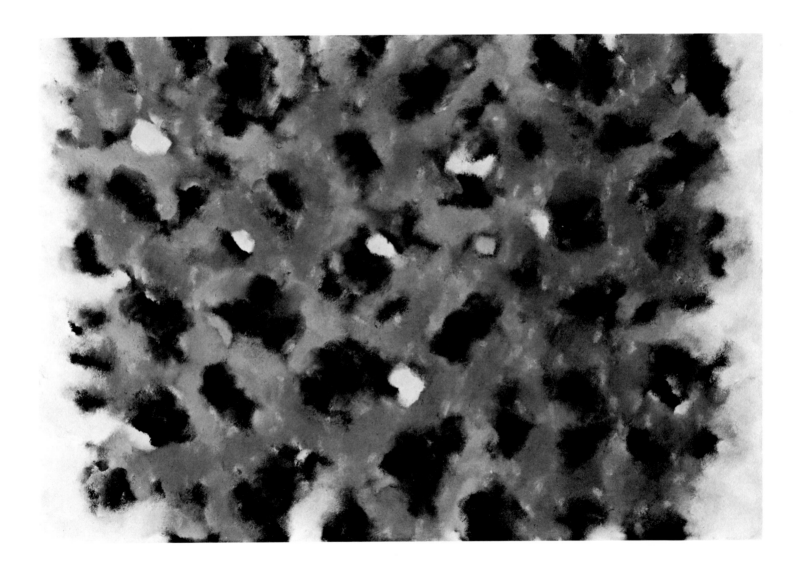

53 *Sky Blue No 3* 1971
oil on canvas
76.2 × 112 cm

37 *Landscape in Red No II*   1971
oil on canvas
152 × 122 cm

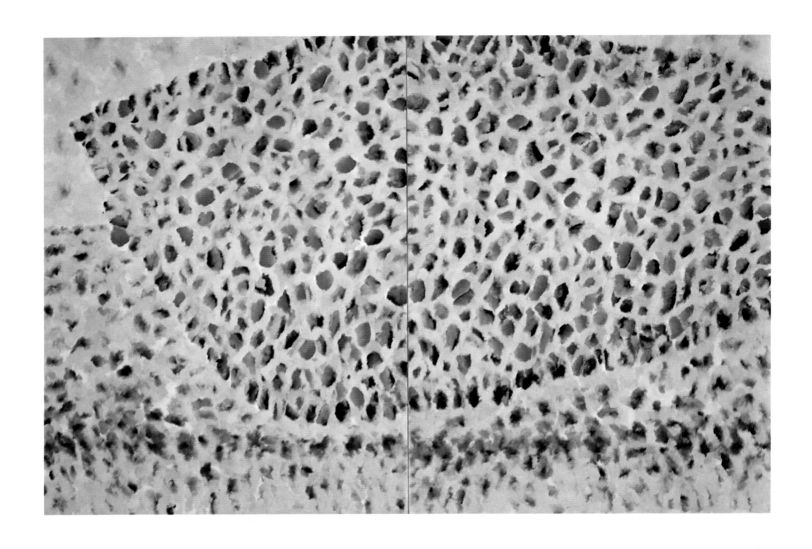

38 *Uplands K* 1972
oil on canvas
228.4 × 355.4 cm

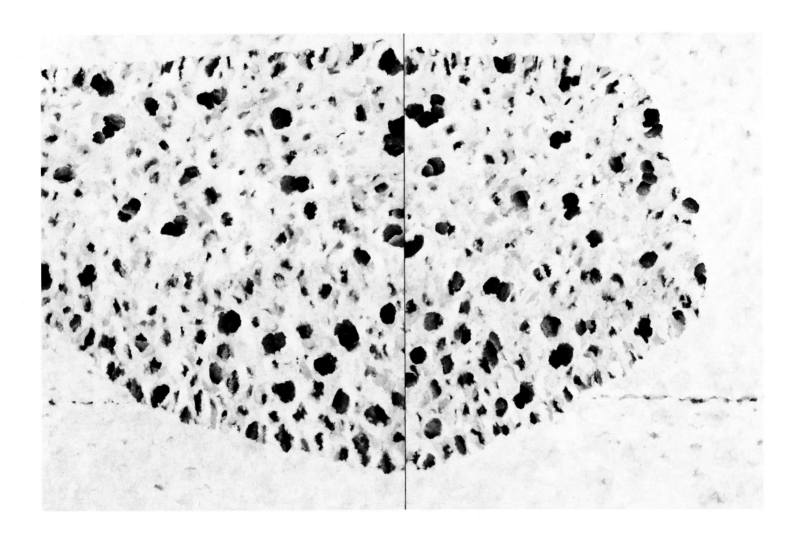

54 *Uplands E*   1971
oil on canvas
228.6 × 355.6 cm (diptych)

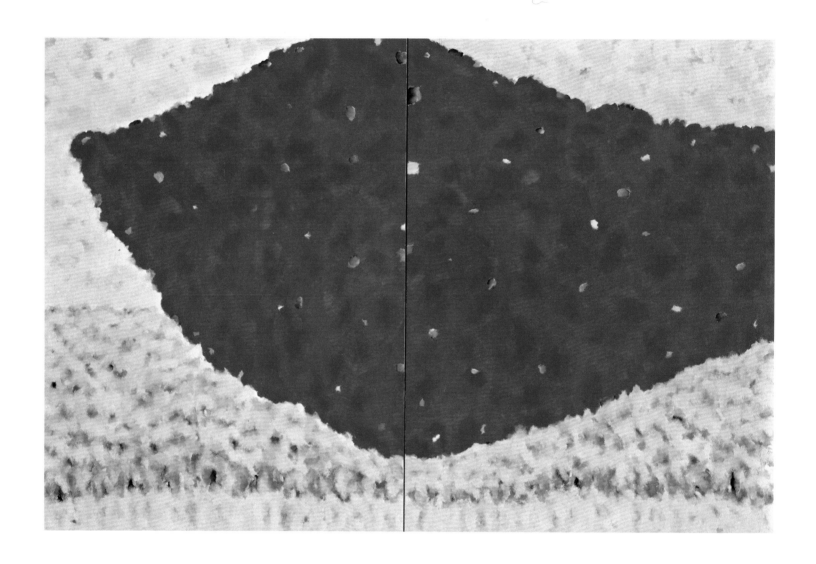

39 *Uplands H*   1972
oil on canvas
182.9 × 241.3 cm (diptych)

40 *Morning Blues* 1972
oil on canvas
139.7 × 114.3 cm

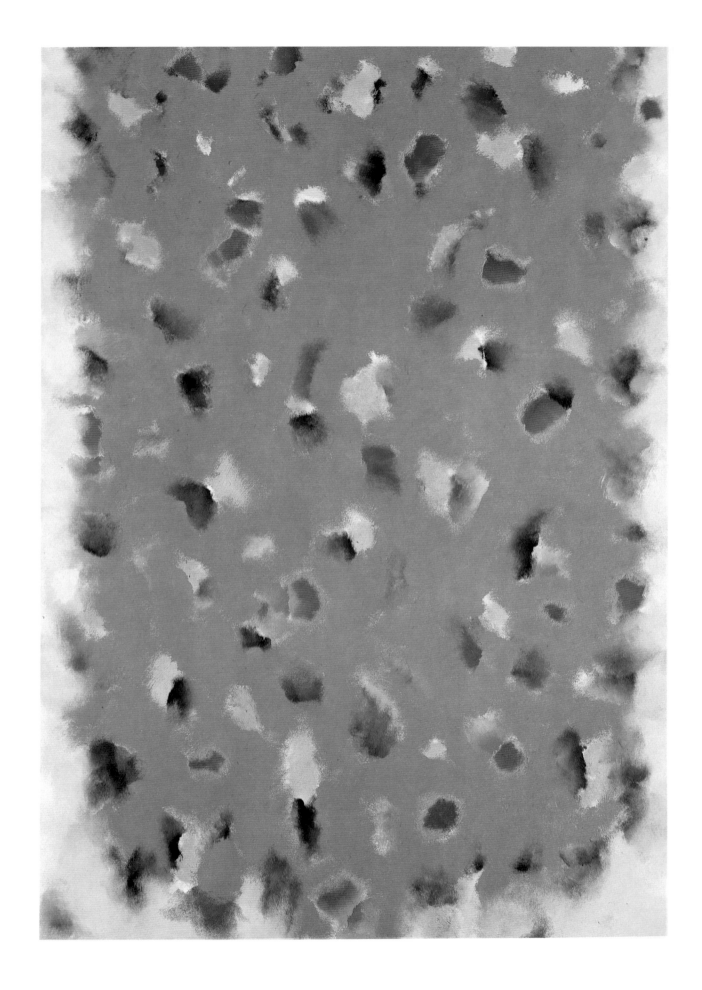

recognized. His participation in the Biennale as Canada's cultural emissary abroad he considered a deep honour. It was his chance to give thanks to a country he had come to love. He had painted its portrait over and over again and internalized its great spaces and dazzling colour. By sheer force of will and imagination he had claimed it for his own; and for once his commitment had been acclaimed by an institution he actually respected.

Iskowitz spent three weeks in Venice during the Biennale, which opened on June 11. Even though he basked in the attention that came his way, it seemed to make him self-conscious, almost embarrassed. In a burst of patriotism he told Peter Mellen, who was in Venice shooting a film about the Biennale: 'Venice is not my kind of thing. I like more excitement – skies, sunrises, sunsets.' Treating Mellen's camera as an inquisitor, he protested that fame would not spoil him. 'The Biennale has nothing to do with my work. Without the Biennale I'd be the same – I'd talk, I'd laugh. The Biennale didn't help my art – but it makes me feel good.' Moos concurred: 'For Gershon the Biennale was a high point. It gave him that added assurance he could do even better art.'

41 *Summer Painting No 2* 1972
oil on canvas
111 × 80 cm

7 COLOUR AND SPACE

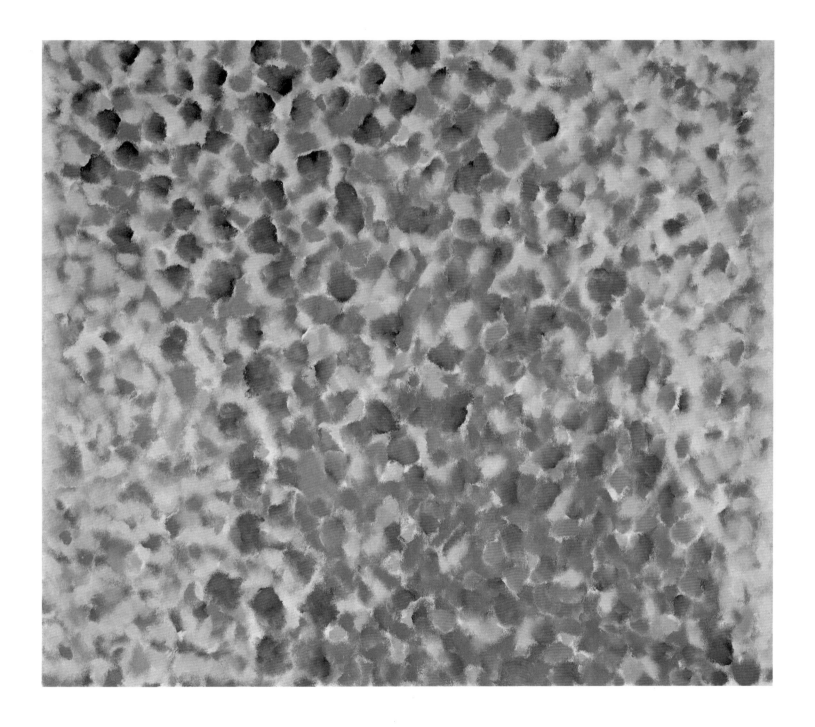

Over a drink at La Cantinetta one night, lapsing into Yiddish, his mother tongue, Iskowitz told a story which could almost be read as a personal manifesto: There was a tailor in Kielce, Moishe-Mendel by name. He had a big gold watch on a chain, of which he was very proud, but he couldn't tell the time. So, when he wore the watch on festive occasions and someone asked him what time it was, he would pull out the watch, flash the face toward his interlocutor, and say, 'Here, look for yourself.'

The greatest compliment one can pay Iskowitz is to listen to what his paintings are saying without trying to force them into a critical vice. And indeed, over the last ten years, their accents have become more marked and their tone more confident and direct. They are about his excitement at discovering a new blue or a new orange, a fresh nuance or shape. They express his passion to communicate his insights to anyone prepared to set aside pre-convictions and embrace that particular vision he has to reveal.

In the seventies, as Moos noted, Iskowitz was propelled into a fresh gust of activity, as though wishing to show that the Biennale had by no means quenched his thirst for self-discovery. He took two more trips north, in 1973 and 1977, both of them to the Yellowknife area, although Churchill has remained his favourite region. His first trip to Yellowknife produced canvases dappled with all-over patterning, titles such as *New Reds*, *New Yellows*, *Orange Blue Mauve*, *New Painting*, and *New Painting in Mauve*, which one critic compared to 'stretched hides from fantasized pintos.' In 1973 he mixed new colours to crown his impressions of Yellowknife, surrounding them with a Hallelujah chorus of attendant colours to enhance their glory. The following year, in works such as *Orange Red Painting* and *Violet Blue Painting*, he turned up the velocity of his painting by introducing more space, thereby breaking up the masses of dense patterning into whirlwinds of colour breaking free of the canvases at the edges. In his Seasons series of 1975 he fused the best elements of the preceding two years – colour and space – and dramatized the tension between them. At this point he felt he had taken the energy of the Uplands period, which began in 1969, to its limit, and again he sought a fresh avenue of expression.

In 1976 he found what he was looking for. He painted two series, the first a set of Variations on grey, red, and deep blue, in which he simplified his paintings by reducing the number of dots on the canvas from tumultuous torrents to minor flurries – a veritable nature in close-up. Then he turned to an investigation of light using deep bold reds and blues as his matrixes, and devoted a series to each colour. The Midnight Blues series is the one he continued

42 *Orange Blue Mauve Painting*   1973
oil on canvas
152.7 × 178.3 cm

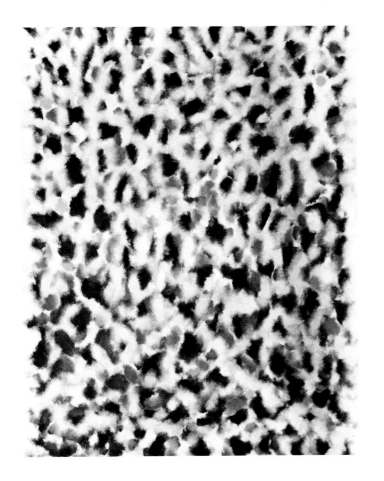

55 *Ultra Blue Green*   1973
oil on canvas
157.6 × 127 cm

56 *Spring*   1974
oil on canvas
153 × 137.5 cm

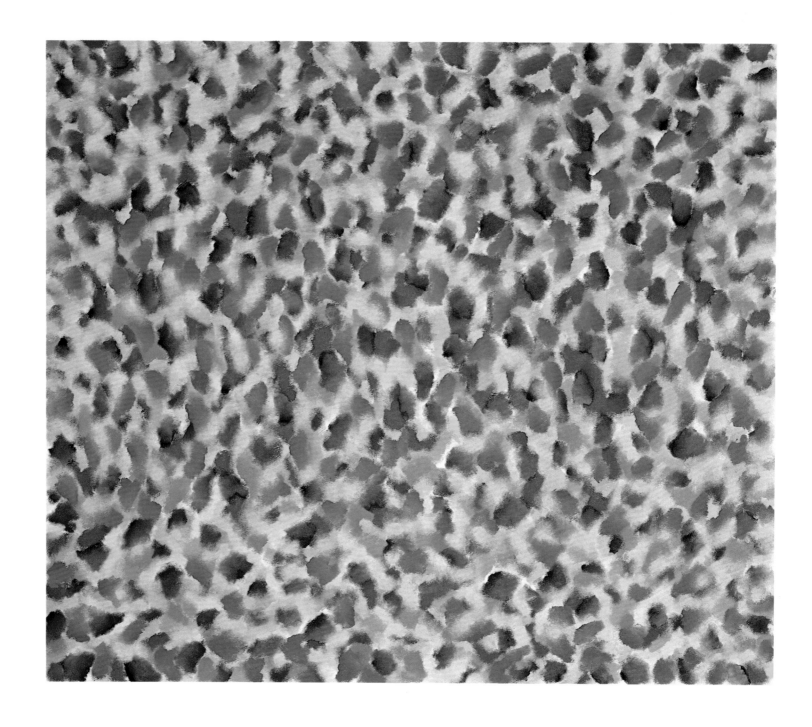

43 *Violet Blue Painting* 1974
oil on canvas
167.6 × 195.6 cm

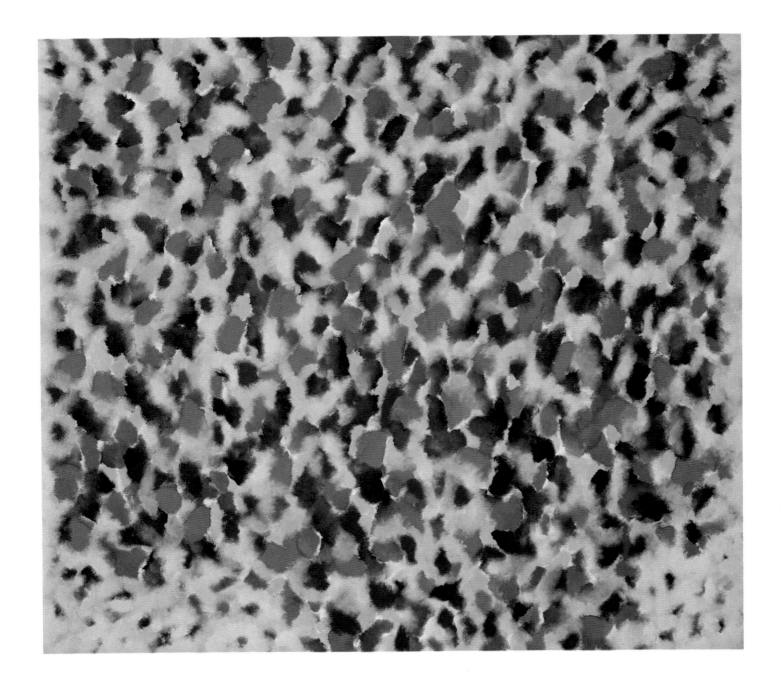

44 *New Green Red Painting*   1974
oil on canvas
167.6 × 195.6 cm

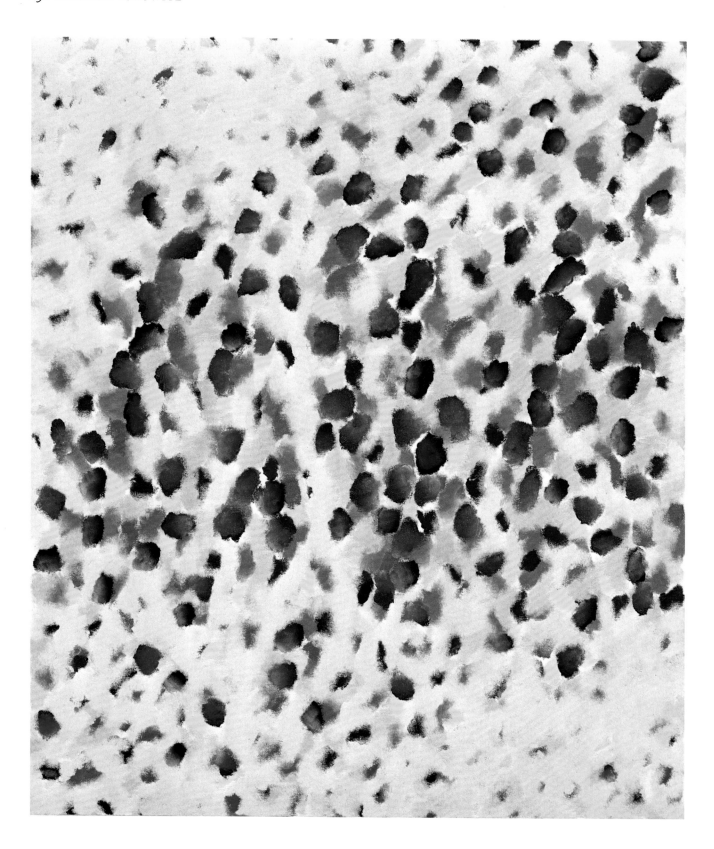

45 *Seasons No 6* 1974
oil on canvas
152.4 × 132.1 cm

46 *Little Orange Painting II* 1975
oil on canvas
177.8 × 165.1 cm

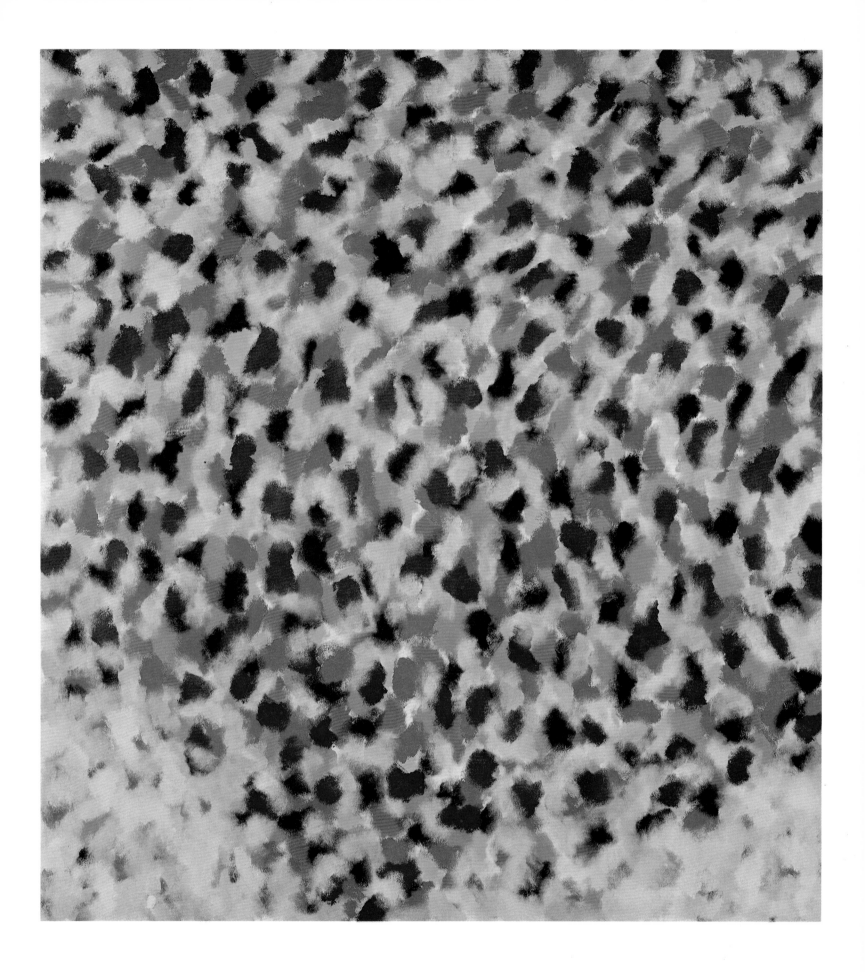

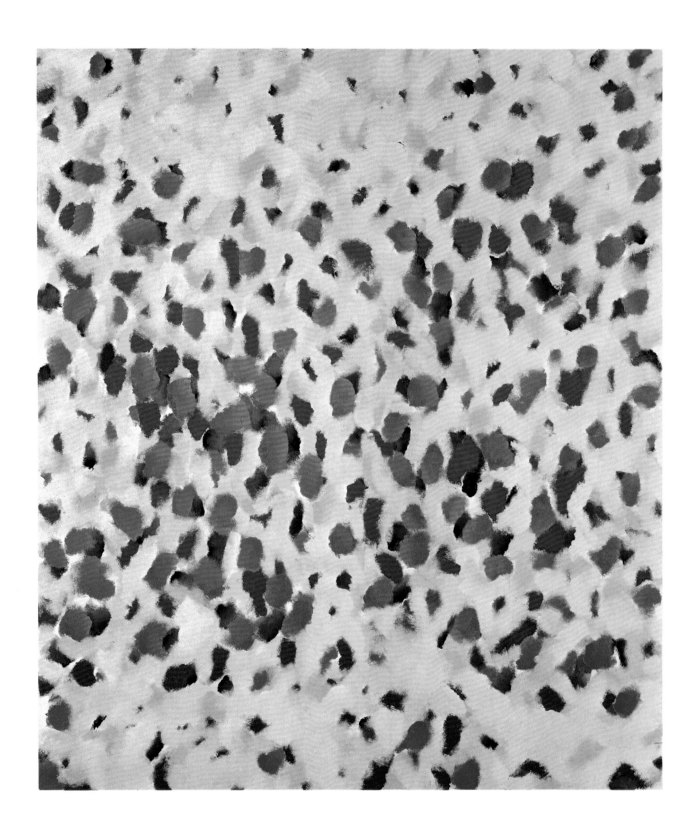

47 *New Orange Red Painting*   1975
oil on canvas
152.5 × 132 cm

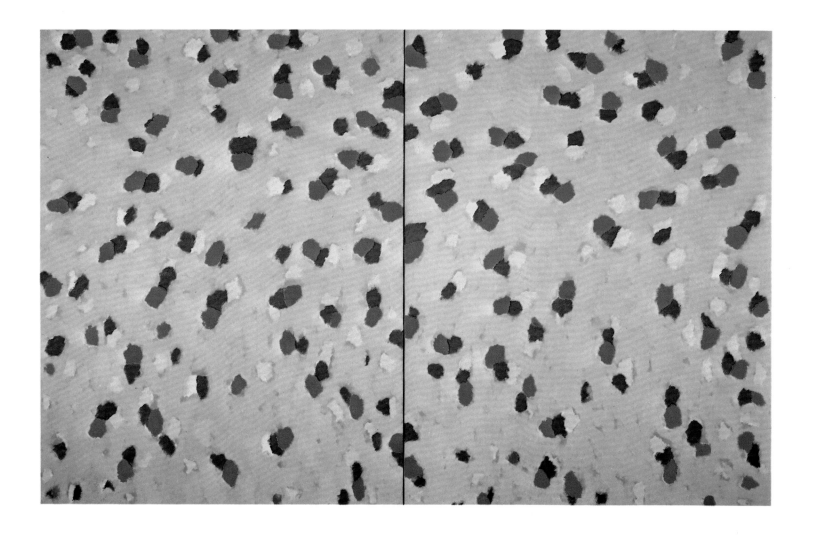

48 *Variations on Green No 3*   1975–76
oil on canvas
123.4 × 335.9 cm

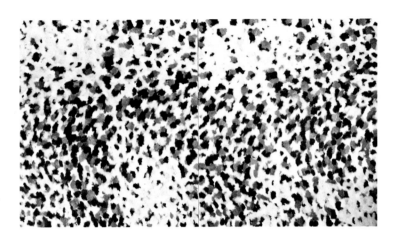

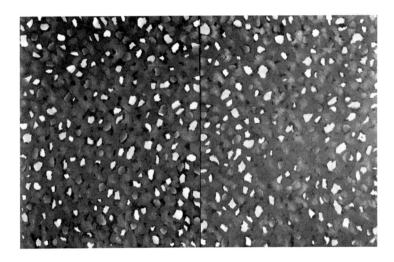

57 *Highlands No 2* 1975–76
oil on canvas
216 × 387 cm (diptych)

58 *Variations on Deep Blues No 3* 1975–76
oil on canvas
223.5 × 355.6 cm (diptych)

59 *Midnight Blue No 7* 1976
oil on canvas
140 × 120 cm

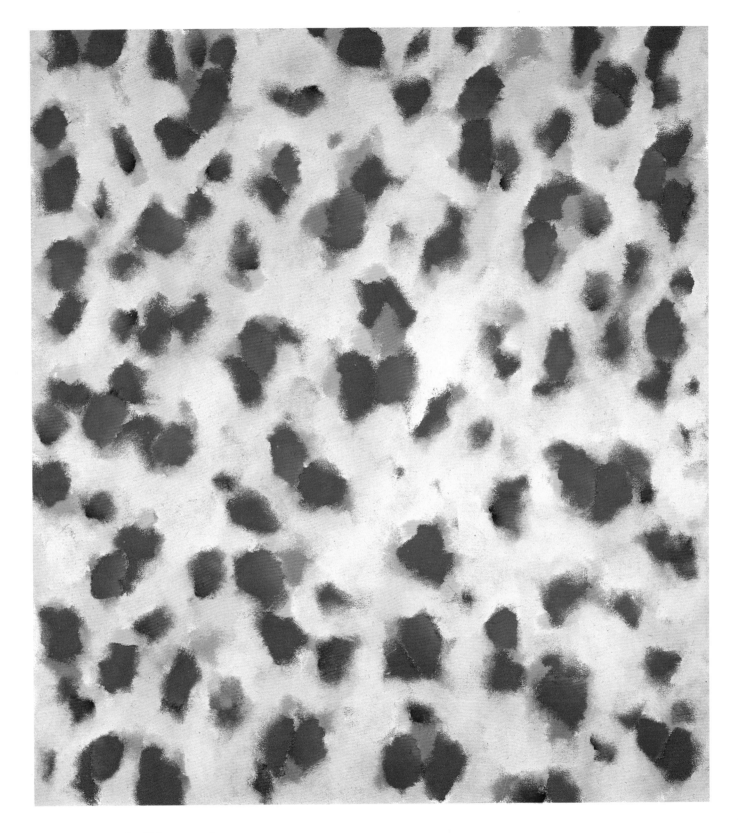

49 *Variations on Red No 7*   1976
oil on canvas
119.4 × 106.7 cm

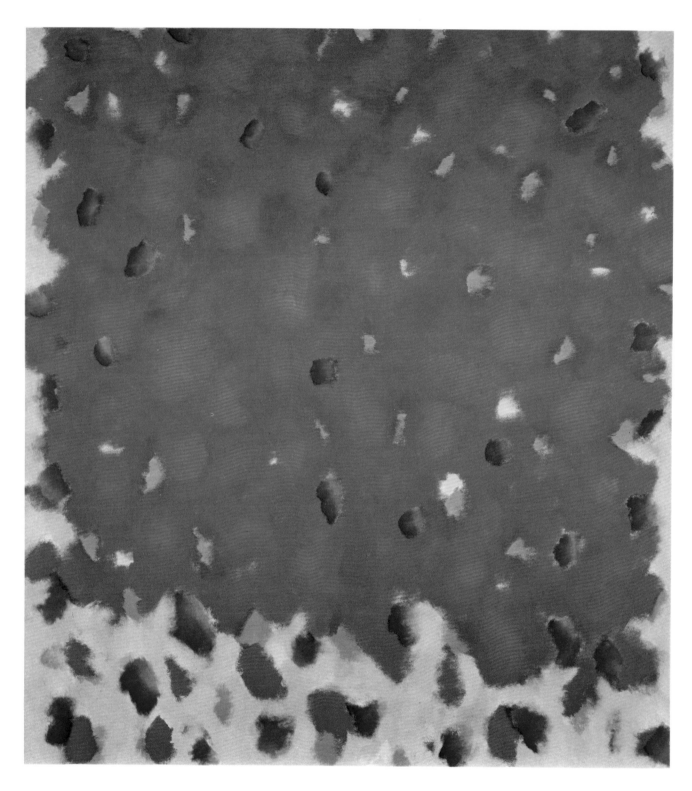

50 *November No 1* 1976
oil on canvas
132 × 119.4 cm

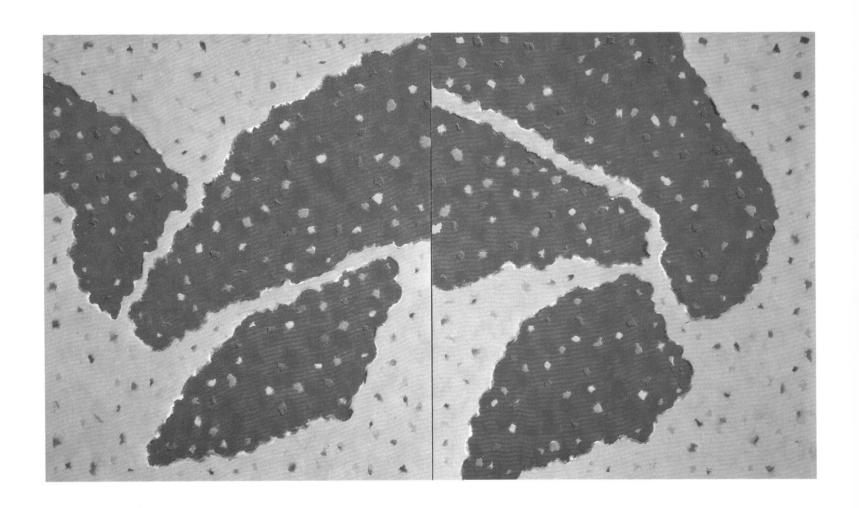

51 *Summer E*   1978
oil on canvas
218.4 × 386.4 cm

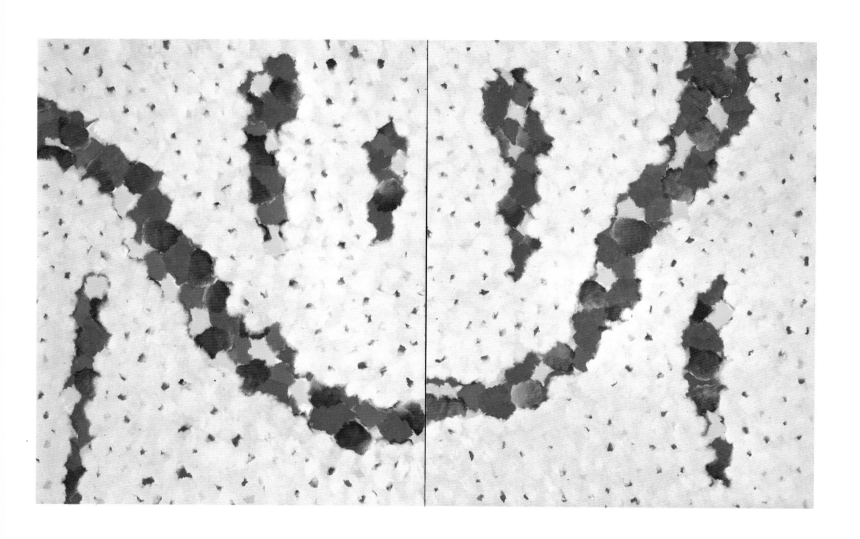

52 *Mauve C* 1979
oil on canvas
203.2 × 345.4 cm

53 *Autumn J* 1978
oil on canvas
96.5 × 81.3 cm

54 *February 6* 1978
water-colour
32.4 × 38 cm

55 *Untitled* 1978
water-colour
55.3 × 32.4 cm

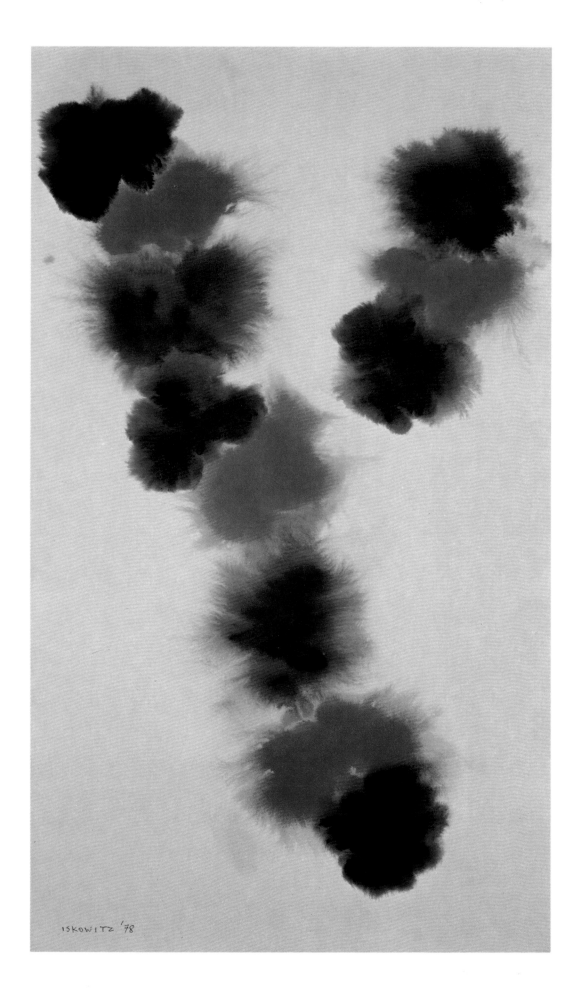

ISKOWITZ '78

to build on. He was pleased with the contrasts between his intensely coloured shapes and the surrounding greyish space. He felt confident enough, especially after his next flight to Yellowknife in 1977, to begin using deep purple and green matrixes blocked out in dense islands and studded with red, blue, yellow, and green dots – as exemplified in his Highlands series. As one thing led unexpectedly to the next, his reds turned into bright pinks and he became fascinated with the qualities of orange. In 1979 and 1980, using compositional ideas he had discovered in the 1977 water-colour series, his shapes became elongated islands and horse-shoes flashing against grey and aqua grounds. Then, in 1981, came another challenge. He wished to convey 'a feeling of the night, a feeling of mystery, with lots of depth, unity, and composition.' *Night Greens D* and *Night Violet A* are two of the strongest oils he has every painted. Jagged lines of yellow and red shoot through glorious coverings of green and purple. In them Iskowitz left the age of light behind and entered the era of electricity.

In 1974 he was elected a member of the Royal Canadian Academy. In 1977 he was awarded a medal in honour of the Queen's silver jubilee. The Canada Council Art Bank has purchased $87,000 worth of his paintings; and in 1977 they included his work in the exhibition, Seven Canadian

60 *Deep Lilac No 2* 1977
oil on canvas
106.5 × 96.5 cm

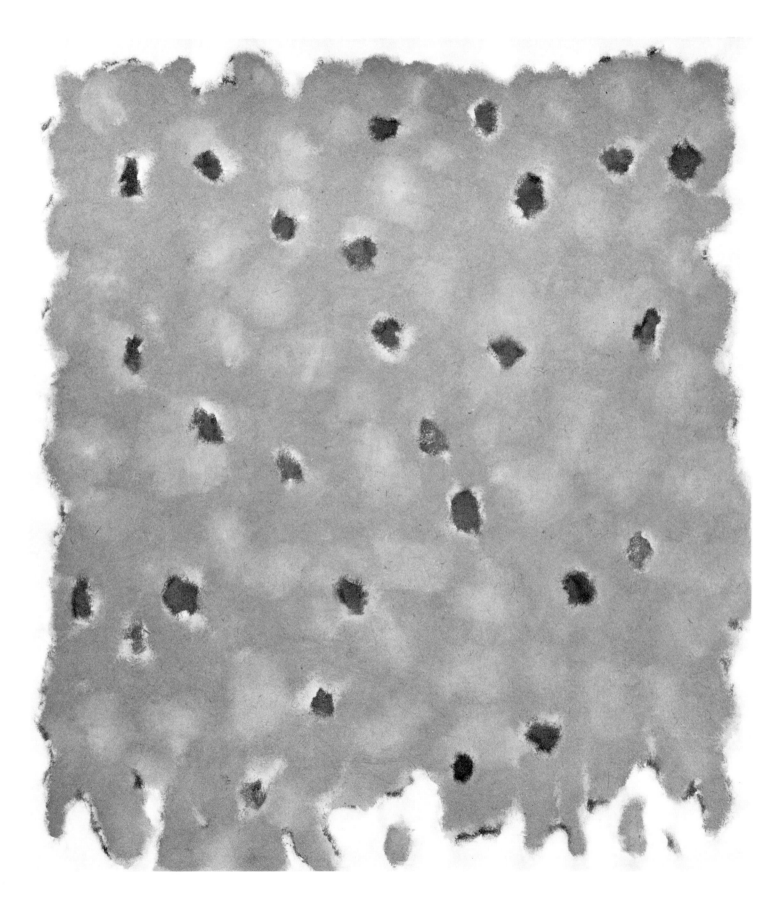

61 *Orange Painting No 1*   1977
oil on canvas
104 × 101.6 cm

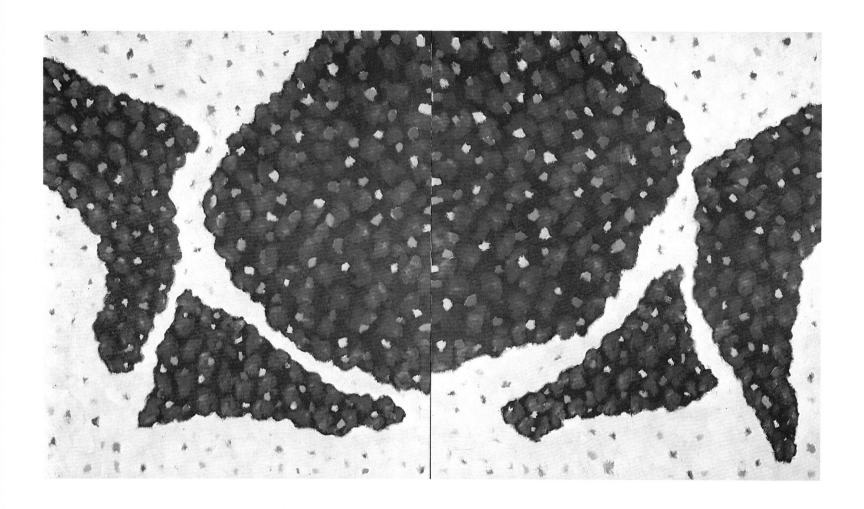

56 *Autumn A*   1978
oil on canvas
218.4 × 386.1 cm

57 *Violet A* 1981
oil on canvas
99.1 × 134.6 cm

Painters, which circulated in New Zealand and Australia. 'The most impressive paintings here are those of Gershon Iskowitz,' wrote one critic in Wellington, pointing to their 'sensitive and lyrical use of colour.' 'Viewed patiently,' wrote another, 'they seem to move, suggesting a wide range of cosmic phenomena, none explicitly stated.' The same year Iskowitz's mastery of colour was praised in New York, where he had his first one-man show at the Martha Jackson Gallery in February.

In May 1980 Iskowitz was included in another traveling group show in New York, selected by Mary Chandor, former assistant curator of the National Gallery, under the sponsorship of Nabisco. 'Canadian artists are, in a number of cases, sophisticated colorists,' wrote David L. Shirey in the *New York Times*, singling out Iskowitz as 'extremely gifted in selecting and arranging lyrically beautiful colors that coalesce into radiant composition.'

It would be wrong to say Toronto has produced a School of Iskowitz; nor has it produced a School of Bush, Rayner, or Town. Toronto is a conglomeration of individual artists who derive from other individual artists; and Iskowitz's painting is closer to that of Matisse, Arshile Gorky, Chaim Soutine, or Monet than that of Graham Coughtry, William Ronald, or Michael Snow. Every aspiring painter, nevertheless, has had to consider his work carefully. He repre-

sents different things to different people. According to Dan Solomon, 'Iskowitz and Jack Bush are the only two people in this town who thought specifically about carefully constructed colour relationships and how paint sits on the surface of a canvas. It's the abstract elements that make his pictures great.' Others cannot help but be moved by his slow, gradual development. 'That approach to me is sanity,' says John MacGregor, and his opinion has been echoed by David Bolduc: 'The continuity within the paintings themselves and the continuity of his life are just an impressive feat. He found something that could take the place of what he lost.'

Bolduc's comment is the key which unlocks Iskowitz's art. Painting is the disciplined human activity with which he searches to unite his present and his past, to bridge the rupture caused by the war. That urge to unify his experience stands behind everything he does, providing an emotional depth to his work which goes far beyond making images of the land from a helicopter window.

His great recuperative effort shows no signs of recession; if anything, it has become stronger with the years. Already he is planning another trip to the north as soon as his retrospective ends. He is still searching for more space, more freedom, both in his art and his life. At the end of October 1981 he surprised everyone by buying a one-

62 *Lilac C*   1978
oil on canvas
96.5 × 81 cm

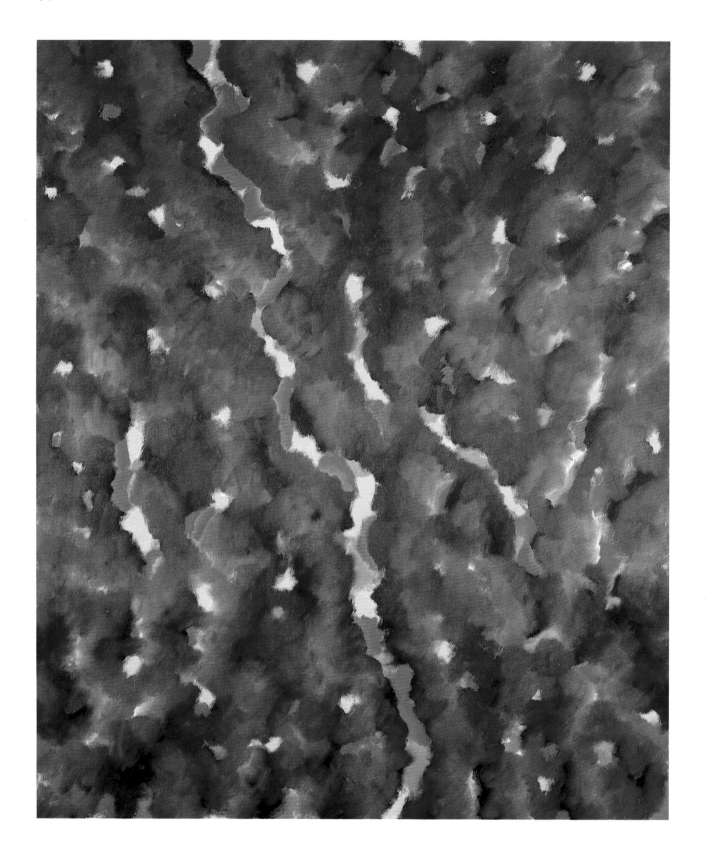

58 *Night Greens D* 1981
oil on canvas
190.5 × 160 cm

59 *Night Violet A* 1981
oil on canvas
190.5 × 160 cm

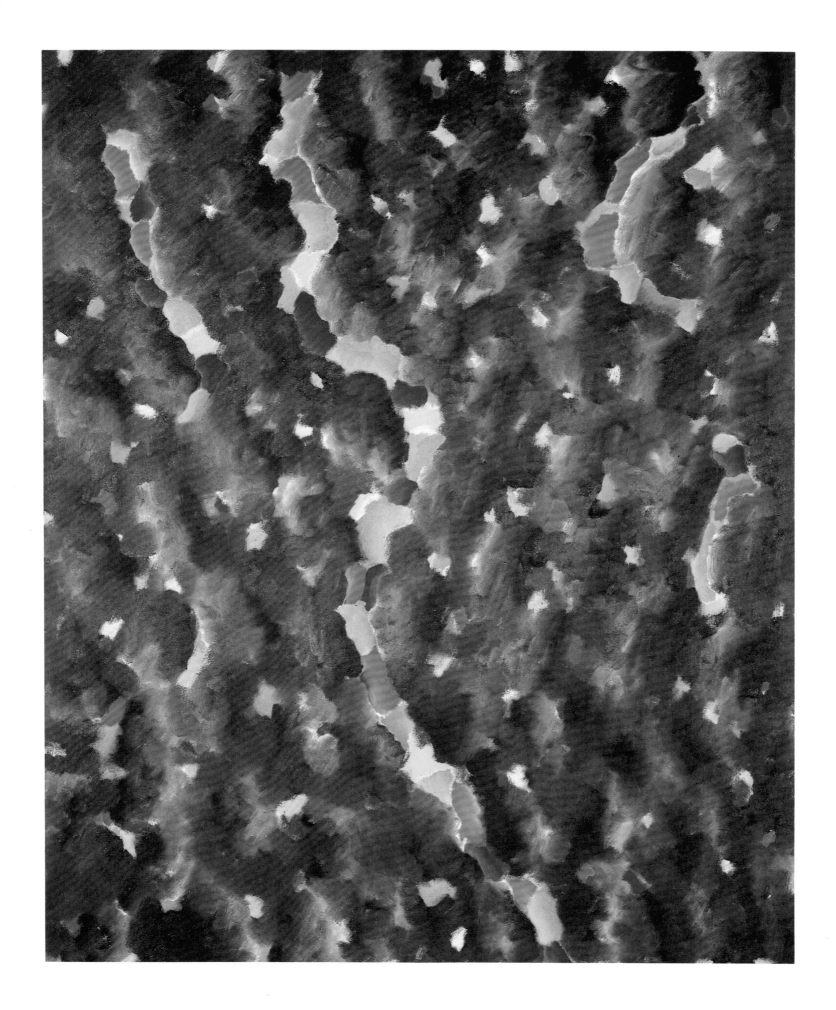

storey studio at King and Tecumseh in Toronto, twice as
large as the one on Spadina and College. His friend Luigi
Orgera found it for him; and the prospect of moving into
his very own stone bunker ignited him into immediate
action – he decided to buy the property five minutes after
first seeing it. The new studio, a handsome white brick
building with seven windows along one side, will be fur-
nished in the same way as the previous one, only there will
be more storage space and a new refrigerator and stove.
Orgera has even planned a rooftop garden complete with
an Italian folly where Iskowitz can relax before he paints.
Since his living space is of such importance to him, the
move to King Street is likely to find its artistic expression in
another blaze of energy and colour.

Throughout his years in Toronto Iskowitz has remained
the *folksman* his father was, liking nothing better than to sit
down with close friends and, looking over his life as from a
great height, to reminisce about those incidents that en-
raged him or gave him pleasure. He does not compare
himself to Rembrandt or Picasso. The only claims he makes
are that his work is honest and makes sense. This criteria
he applies to the work of other artists as well. With respect
to young artists his attitude is always 'Wait and see' –
which expresses the value he places on continuity and
hard work.

63 *Untitled drawing*   1980
felt pen
48 × 62 cm

64 *Untitled drawing*   1980
felt pen
48 × 62 cm

65 *Untitled drawing*   1980
felt pen
48 × 62 cm

66 *Untitled drawing*   1980
felt pen
48 × 62 cm

63

65

64

66

67 Iskowitz in front of Tecumseh Street studio, 1981

As Iskowitz grows older (he turned sixty in November 1981), and perhaps because he is childless, he has become more concerned with handing down his legacy to future generations. He expresses this like a rabbi delivering an elliptical sermon, but in the context of his life experience every word is telling: 'It's very important to give something so the next generation can really believe in something. I think the artist works for himself for the most part. Every artist goes through stages of fear and love or whatever it is and has to fight day after day to survive like everyone else. Art is a form of satisfying yourself and satisfying others. We want to be good and belong. That goes through history; we're striving for it.'

SELECT BIBLIOGRAPHY

MISCELLANEOUS DOCUMENTATION

'Interview with Gershon Iskowitz.' CBC Radio Programme, 1969, Toronto

'Standing Apart: Gershon Iskowitz.' Filmed at the 36th Venice Biennale, 1972. Produced by Peter and Fran Mellen

'I Paint What I Know: Gerson Iskowitz.' Filmed in Toronto for ETV Channel 19, 1972. Supervised by Peter Mellen

'Gershon Iskowitz.' Filmed by CTV Channel 9 for the programme 'W-5,' 1973

'Gershon Iskowitz.' Videotape produced by York University, 1975

ARTICLES

Freedman, Adele. 'Gerson Iskowitz: Colors of Joy from the Heart of Darkness.' *Toronto Life*, October 1977, 186–9

Heinrich, Theodore Allen. 'The Intimate Cartography of Gershon Iskowitz's Painting.' *artscanada*, XXXIV, 2, May/June 1977, 12–17

Mellen, Peter. 'Gershon Iskowitz.' *artscanada*, XXVIII, 5, October/November 1971, 48–53

Nasgaard, Roald. 'Gershon Iskowitz.' *artscanada*, XXX, 3, August 1973, 56–9

EXHIBITIONS

ONE-MAN EXHIBITIONS

1960–1	Here & Now Gallery, Toronto, Ontario
1961	YMHA, Toronto, Ontario
1961	Victoria College, University of Toronto, Toronto, Ontario
1963	Dorothy Cameron Gallery, Toronto, Ontario
1964	Gallery Moos, Toronto, Ontario
1966	Gallery Moos, Toronto, Ontario
1967	Waterloo University, Waterloo, Ontario (Retrospective Exhibition)
1967	Gallery Moos, Toronto, Ontario
1969	Gallery Moos, Toronto, Ontario
1970	Gallery Moos, Toronto, Ontario
1971	Gallery Moos, Toronto, Ontario
1973	Hart House, University of Toronto, Toronto, Ontario
1973	Gallery Moos, Toronto, Ontario
1973	Rodman Hall Arts Centre, St Catharines, Ontario
1974	Galerie Allen, Vancouver, British Columbia
1974	Gallery Moos, Toronto, Ontario
1975	Glenbow-Alberta Institute, Calgary, Alberta
1975	Gallery Moos, Toronto, Ontario
1976	Owens Art Gallery, Mount Allison University, Sackville, New Brunswick
1976	Canadian Art Galleries, Calgary, Alberta
1976	Gallery Moos, Toronto, Ontario
1977	Martha Jackson Gallery, New York, New York
1977	Art Gallery of Nova Scotia, Halifax, Nova Scotia
1977	Gallery Moos, Toronto, Ontario
1978	Gallery Moos, Toronto, Ontario
1979	Thomas Gallery, Winnipeg, Manitoba
1979	Gallery Moos, Calgary, Alberta
1979	Gallery Moos, Toronto, Ontario
1980	Robertson Galleries, Ottawa, Ontario
1981	Gallery Moos, Toronto, Ontario

GROUP EXHIBITIONS

1957	Isaacs Gallery, Toronto, Ontario
1957	Hayter Gallery, Toronto, Ontario
1958	Jordan Gallery, Toronto, Ontario
1959	Gallery Moos, Toronto, Ontario
1964	Winnipeg Biennial, Winnipeg, Manitoba
1965	vith Canadian Biennial, National Gallery of Canada, Ottawa, Ontario
1966	Winnipeg Biennial, Winnipeg, Manitoba
1967	Ontario Centennial Art Exhibition, traveling exhibition throughout Ontario organized by the Province of Ontario
1970	'Eight Artists from Canada,' Tel Aviv Museum, Tel Aviv, Israel
1971	Man and His World, Montreal, Quebec
1972	xxxvi International Biennial Exhibition of Art, Venice, Italy
1972	'Toronto Painters 1953–65,' National Gallery of Canada, Ottawa, Ontario and the Art Gallery of Ontario, Toronto, Ontario
1973	'The Canadian Canvas,' traveling exhibition organized by Time Canada

1977	'Seven Canadian Painters,' Canada Council Art Bank, traveling exhibition throughout New Zealand and Australia
1978	'A Toronto Sensibility,' The Art Gallery at Harbourfront, Toronto, Ontario
1979	'Now and Then,' Factory 77, Toronto, Ontario
1979	'Compass / 8 Painters,' The Art Gallery at Harbourfront, Toronto, Ontario
1980	'Contemporary Canadian Art,' Nabisco World Headquarters Reception Gallery, East Hanover, New York
1980	'A Selection of Canadian Paintings,' The Art Gallery at Harbourfront, Toronto, Ontario
1980	'The Staff Collects – An Experiment,' paintings from the Shell Collection, The Art Gallery at Harbourfront, Toronto, Ontario
1981	'Other Places, Other Painters; Canadian Contemporary Art,' Sir George Williams Art Gallery, Concordia University, Montreal, Quebec

NOTES ON ILLUSTRATIONS

COLOUR PLATES

1 *Night Blues B*   1981
oil on canvas
116.2 × 99.1 cm
Private Collection
Photography: T.E. Moore, Toronto
p. ii

2 *Orange B*   1980
oil on canvas
91.4 × 86.4 cm
Mrs Ellen Melas Kryiazi,
Lausanne, Switzerland
Photography: Art Gallery of
Ontario, Toronto
p. 7

3 *Highland in Orange No 2*   1977
oil on canvas
167.5 × 183 cm
Lavalin Incorporated, Montreal
Photography: Art Gallery of
Ontario, Toronto
p. 8

4 *Highland in Green No 2*   1977
oil on canvas
106.7 × 96.5 cm
Citibank Canada, Toronto
Photography: Art Gallery of
Ontario, Toronto
p. 9

5 *Newscape*   1976
oil on canvas
152 × 208 cm
Private Collection
Photography: Art Gallery of
Ontario, Toronto
p. 10

6 *Red F*   1979
oil on canvas
160 × 137.2 cm
Heather Reisman, Montreal
Photography: Brian Merrett,
Montreal
p. 11

7 *Deep Red No 6*   1976
oil on canvas
195.6 × 228.6 cm
Richard J. Roberts and Garth H.
Drabinsky, Toronto
Photography: T.E. Moore, Toronto
p. 13

8 *Uplands B*   1969–70
oil on canvas
213.4 × 355.3 cm (diptych)
Gallery Moos, Toronto
Photography: Art Gallery of
Ontario, Toronto
p. 14

9 *Water Carrier*   1952
gouache on board
29.8 × 39.4 cm
Arthur Hammond, Toronto
Photography: Art Gallery of
Ontario, Toronto
p. 21

10 *Side Street*   1952
water-colour on board
50.8 × 61 cm
Gallery Moos, Toronto
Photography: Art Gallery of
Ontario, Toronto
p. 25

11 *Torah*   1951
gouache on board
43.2 × 53.3 cm
Gallery Moos, Toronto
Photography: Art Gallery of
Ontario, Toronto
p. 33

12 *Buchenwald*   1944–45
water-colour and ink
38.1 × 50.8 cm
Arthur Hammond, Toronto
Photography: Art Gallery of
Ontario, Toronto
p. 45

13 *Self Portrait*   1947
oil on canvas laid on board
50.8 × 40.6 cm
Gallery Moos, Toronto
Photography: Art Gallery of
Ontario, Toronto
p. 60

14 *Apple Orchard*   1952
oil on canvas laid on board
40.6 × 50.8 cm
Gallery Moos, Toronto
Photography: Art Gallery of
Ontario, Toronto
p. 64

15 *Yzkor*   1952
water-colour and ink
30.5 × 40.6 cm
Gallery Moos, Toronto
Photography: Art Gallery of
Ontario, Toronto
p. 65

16 *Miriam*   1952
   gouache on board
   38.1 × 26.7 cm
   Gallery Moos, Toronto
   Photography: T.E. Moore, Toronto
   p. 68

17 *Sunset*   1960
   oil on canvas
   127 × 101.6 cm
   Gallery Moos, Toronto
   Photography: Art Gallery of
   Ontario, Toronto
   p. 88

18 *Autumn Reflections*   1962
   oil on canvas
   125.4 × 100 cm
   Private Collection
   Photography: Art Gallery of
   Ontario, Toronto
   p. 89

19 *Sunset*   1962
   water-colour
   24 × 33.5 cm
   Private Collection
   Photography: Art Gallery of
   Ontario, Toronto
   p. 92

20 *Spring*   1962
   oil on canvas
   165.4 × 140 cm
   The Bank of Canada, Ottawa
   Photography: John Evans, Ottawa
   p. 97

21 *Self Portrait*   1963
   water-colour
   71.1 × 50.8 cm
   Tony and Shirley Stapells, Toronto
   Photography: Art Gallery of
   Ontario, Toronto
   p. 98

22 *Seated Figure*   1964
   oil on canvas
   68.6 × 58.4 cm
   Dr Jerry and Shirley Giblon, Toronto
   Photography: Art Gallery of
   Ontario, Toronto
   p. 99

23 *Untitled*   1964
   oil on canvas
   50.8 × 76.2 cm
   Joel Siegel, Toronto
   Photography: Art Gallery of
   Ontario, Toronto
   p. 102

24. *Autumn Images*   1965
   oil on canvas
   76.2 × 61 cm
   Jacob and Dorothy Hendeles,
   Toronto
   Photography: Art Gallery of
   Ontario, Toronto
   p. 103

25 *Autumn Sky*   1964
   water-colour
   71.1 × 88.9 cm
   Tony and Shirley Stapells, Toronto
   Photography: Art Gallery of
   Ontario, Toronto
   p. 104

26 *Parry Sound Variations*   1965
   water-colour
   58.4 × 45.7 cm
   Dr Jerry and Shirley Giblon, Toronto
   Photography: Art Gallery of
   Ontario, Toronto
   p. 105

27 *Parry Sound*   1965
   water-colour
   66 × 78.1 cm
   Tony and Shirley Stapells, Toronto
   Photography: Art Gallery of
   Ontario, Toronto
   p. 106

28 *Sextet*   1965
   oil on canvas
   152.5 × 122 cm
   Private Collection
   Photography: Art Gallery of
   Ontario, Toronto
   p. 107

29 *Summer Sounds*   1965
   oil on canvas
   172.7 × 139.7 cm
   Art Gallery of Ontario, Toronto
   Photography: Art Gallery of
   Ontario, Toronto
   p. 108

30 *Summer Blues*   1966
   oil on canvas
   81.3 × 101.6 cm
   Mr and Mrs J.T. McLeod, Toronto
   Photography: Art Gallery of
   Ontario, Toronto
   p. 110

31 *Summer Skies*   1966
oil on canvas
102 × 82 cm
Crown Life Collection of Canadian
Art, Toronto
Photography: Art Gallery of
Ontario, Toronto
p. 111

32 *Autumn Landscape No 6*   1967
oil on canvas
152.4 × 122 cm
Toronto Dominion Bank, Toronto
Photography: VIDA/Saltmarche,
Toronto
p. 114

33 *Autumn Landscape No 5*   1967
oil on canvas
152.4 × 127 cm
Gallery Moos, Toronto
Photography: Art Gallery of
Ontario, Toronto
p. 115

34 *Seasons No I*   1968–69
oil on canvas
254 × 355.6 cm (diptych)
National Gallery of Canada, Ottawa
p. 117

35 *Lowlands No 13*   1970
oil on canvas
152.4 × 121.9 cm
Mr and Mrs Jules Loeb, Toronto
Photography: Art Gallery of
Ontario, Toronto
p. 118

36 *Triptych*   1969–70
oil on canvas
274.3 × 139.7; 304.8 × 152.4;
274.3 × 139.7 cm
Gallery Moos, Toronto
Photography: T.E Moore, Toronto
p. 120

37 *Landscape in Red No II*   1971
oil on canvas
152 × 122 cm
Carmen Lamanna, Toronto
Photography: Art Gallery of
Ontario, Toronto
p. 123

38 *Uplands K*   1972
oil on canvas
228.4 × 355.4 cm
Art Gallery of Hamilton, Hamilton
Gift of Mr John Morris Thurston and
Wintario, 1977
Photography: Art Gallery of
Ontario, Toronto
p. 124

39 *Uplands H*   1972
oil on canvas
182.9 × 241.3 cm (diptych)
Art Gallery of Ontario, Toronto
Purchased with the assistance of
Wintario, 1977
Photography: Art Gallery of
Ontario, Toronto
p. 126

40 *Morning Blues*   1972
oil on canvas
139.7 × 114.3 cm
Eugene and Margaret Sawkiw,
Toronto
Photography: Art Gallery of
Ontario, Toronto
p. 127

41 *Summer Painting No 2*   1972
oil on canvas
111 × 80 cm
Peter and Enid MacLachlan, Toronto
Photography: Art Gallery of
Ontario, Toronto
p. 128

42 *Orange Blue Mauve Painting*   1973
oil on canvas
152.7 × 178.3 cm
The Robert McLaughlin Gallery,
Oshawa
Photography: Art Gallery of
Ontario, Toronto
p. 131

43 *Violet Blue Painting*   1974
oil on canvas
167.6 × 195.6 cm
Gallery Moos, Toronto
Photography: Art Gallery of
Ontario, Toronto
p. 134

44 *New Green Red Painting*   1974
oil on canvas
167.6 × 195.6 cm
Mr and Mrs Irving Waltman,
Toronto
Photography: Art Gallery of
Ontario, Toronto
p. 135

45 *Seasons No 6*   1974
oil on canvas
152.4 × 132.1 cm
Private Collection
Photography: Art Gallery of
Ontario, Toronto
p. 136

46 *Little Orange Painting II*   1975
oil on canvas
177.8 × 165.1 cm
Art Gallery of Ontario, Toronto
Gift of Beverly and Boris Zerafa,
1975
Photography: Art Gallery of
Ontario, Toronto
p. 137

47 *New Orange Red Painting*   1975
oil on canvas
152.5 × 132 cm
The Canada Council Art Bank,
Ottawa
Photography: John Evans, Ottawa
p. 138

48 *Variations on Green No 3*   1975–76
oil on canvas
123.4 × 335.9 cm
The Canada Council Art Bank,
Ottawa
Photography: John Evans, Ottawa
p. 139

49 *Variations on Red No 7*   1976
oil on canvas
119.4 × 106.7 cm
David and Anita Blackwood, Port
Hope
Photography: Art Gallery of
Ontario, Toronto
p. 141

50 *November No 1*   1976
oil on canvas
132 × 119.4 cm
Art Gallery of Windsor, Windsor
Gift from the Queen's Jubilee Art
Collection through the Province of
Ontario, 1978
Photography: Art Gallery of
Ontario, Toronto
p. 142

51 *Summer E*   1978
oil on canvas
218.4 × 386.4 cm
Gallery Moos, Toronto
Photography: T.E. Moore, Toronto
p. 143

52 *Mauve C*   1979
oil on canvas
203.2 × 345.4 cm
Gallery Moos, Toronto
Photography: T.E. Moore, Toronto
p. 144

53 *Autumn J*   1978
oil on canvas
96.5 × 81.3 cm
Mr and Mrs James H. Morlock,
Toronto
Photography: Art Gallery of
Ontario, Toronto
p. 145

54 *February 6*   1978
water-colour
32.4 × 38 cm
E.A. Magner, Toronto
Photography: Art Gallery of
Ontario, Toronto
p. 146

55 *Untitled*   1978
water-colour
55.3 × 32.4 cm
Marilyn Schiff, Toronto
Photography: Art Gallery of
Ontario, Toronto
p. 147

56 *Autumn A*   1978
oil on canvas
218.4 × 386.1 cm
Gallery Moos, Toronto
Photography: T.E. Moore, Toronto
p. 150

57 *Violet A*   1981
oil on canvas
99.1 × 134.6 cm
Gerald W. Schwartz, Winnipeg
Photography: Brian Merrett,
Montreal
p. 151

58 *Night Greens D*   1981
oil on canvas
190.5 × 160 cm
Gallery Moos, Toronto
Photography: Art Gallery of
Ontario, Toronto
p. 154

59 *Night Violet A*   1981
oil on canvas
190.5 × 160 cm
Gallery Moos, Toronto
Photography: T.E. Moore, Toronto
p. 155

BLACK AND WHITE ILLUSTRATIONS

1 *Luigi Orgera* 1980
felt pen
42.5 × 35 cm
Private Collection
p. 6

2 *Dybbuk* 1947
water-colour and ink
26.7 × 36.8 cm
Gallery Moos, Toronto
Photography: Art Gallery of
Ontario, Toronto
p. 18

3 Grandfather and two aunts, p. 22

4 House on Leśna Street where
Iskowitz lived and had his first
studio, p. 23

5 Front row: Yosl, Gershon and Itchen
Back row: Zisl and Yankl
p. 24

6 Zisl and niece, p. 27

7 *Market* 1953–54
gouache on board
50.8 × 61 cm
Gallery Moos, Toronto
Photography: Art Gallery of
Ontario, Toronto
p. 28

8 *Burning Synagogue* 1953
gouache on board
48.3 × 35.6 cm
Gallery Moos, Toronto
Photography: Art Gallery of
Ontario, Toronto
p. 30

9 *Memory (Mother and Child)* 1951
water-colour and ink
50.8 × 24.3 cm
Gallery Moos, Toronto
Photography: Art Gallery of
Ontario, Toronto
p. 31

10 *Hunger* 1951
water-colour and ink
51 × 33 cm
Gallery Moos, Toronto
Photography: Art Gallery of
Ontario, Toronto
p. 31

11 Family and friends before the war,
p. 32

12 *Ghetto* 1947
water-colour and ink
35.6 × 48.3 cm
Gallery Moos, Toronto
Photography: Art Gallery of
Ontario, Toronto
p. 34

13 *Burning Town* 1952
gouache on board
30.5 × 40.6 cm
Gallery Moos, Toronto
Photography: Art Gallery of
Ontario, Toronto
p. 35

14 *Action* 1941
water-colour and ink
38.1 × 55.9 cm
Gallery Moos, Toronto
Photography: Art Gallery of
Ontario, Toronto
p. 36

15 *Selection Auschwitz* 1947
water-colour and ink
40.6 × 50.8 cm
Gallery Moos, Toronto
Photography: Art Gallery of
Ontario, Toronto
p. 41

16 *Moon: Buchenwald* 1952
oil on board
25.4 × 34.3 cm
Gallery Moos, Toronto
Photography: Art Gallery of
Ontario, Toronto
p. 43

17 *Condemned* 1945
water-colour and ink
68.6 × 50.8 cm
Gallery Moos, Toronto
Photography: Art Gallery of
Ontario, Toronto
p. 44

18 *Escape* 1948
oil on canvas laid on corrugated
paper
36.8 × 45.7 cm
Gallery Moos, Toronto
Photography: Art Gallery of
Ontario, Toronto
p. 46

19 Iskowitz and painting of poet
I.L. Peretz, 1946, p. 49

20 *Waiting* 1947
water-colour and ink on board
41.9 × 54.6 cm
Gallery Moos, Toronto
Photography: Art Gallery of
Ontario, Toronto
p. 51

21 *Action* 1948
oil on canvas laid on board
40.6 × 58.4 cm
Gallery Moos, Toronto
Photography: Art Gallery of
Ontario, Toronto
p. 53

22 *Through Life* 1947
water-colour and ink on board
54.6 × 32.3 cm
Gallery Moos, Toronto
Photography: Art Gallery of
Ontario, Toronto
p. 54

23 *Barracks* 1947
water-colour and ink
38.1 × 50.8 cm
Gallery Moos, Toronto
Photography: Art Gallery of
Ontario, Toronto
p. 56

24 *Yzkor* 1949
gouache on board
30.5 × 40.6 cm
Gallery Moos, Toronto
Photography: Art Gallery of
Ontario, Toronto
p. 57

25 *The Artist's Mother* 1947
oil on canvas laid on board
50.8 × 40.6 cm
Gallery Moos, Toronto
Photography: Art Gallery of
Ontario, Toronto
p. 58

26 *It Burns* 1952
gouache on board
50.8 × 66 cm
Gallery Moos, Toronto
Photography: Art Gallery of
Ontario, Toronto
p. 67

27 *Barrier* 1952
gouache on board
50.8 × 61 cm
Gallery Moos, Toronto
Photography: Art Gallery of
Ontario, Toronto
p. 70

28 *The Wall* 1952
water-colour and ink
59.7 × 45.7 cm
Gallery Moos, Toronto
Photography: Art Gallery of
Ontario, Toronto
p. 71

29 *Explosion* 1952
gouache on board
50.8 × 63.5 cm
Gallery Moos, Toronto
Photography: Art Gallery of
Ontario, Toronto
p. 72

30 *Untitled* 1952
felt pen
21.1 × 27.9 cm
Gallery Moos, Toronto
Photography: Art Gallery of
Ontario, Toronto
p. 73

31 *Untitled* 1952
felt pen
21.1 × 27.9 cm
Gallery Moos, Toronto
Photography: Art Gallery of
Ontario, Toronto
p. 73

32 *Untitled* 1952
felt pen
21.1 × 27.9 cm
Gallery Moos, Toronto
Photography: Art Gallery of
Ontario, Toronto
p. 73

33 *Untitled* 1952
felt pen
21.1 × 27.9 cm
Gallery Moos, Toronto
Photography: Art Gallery of
Ontario, Toronto
p. 73

34 *Untitled* 1952
felt pen
27.9 × 21.1 cm
Gallery Moos, Toronto
Photography: Art Gallery of
Ontario, Toronto
p. 74

35 *Untitled* 1952
felt pen
21.1 × 27.9 cm
Gallery Moos, Toronto
Photography: Art Gallery of
Ontario, Toronto
p. 74

36 Iskowitz, Borden Street
Photography: Michel Lambeth
Toronto
p. 75

37 *Eric Freifeld* 1955
oil on board
50.8 × 38.1 cm
Gallery Moos, Toronto
Photography: Art Gallery of
Ontario, Toronto
p. 77

38 *Landscape* 1954
oil on board
29.7 × 35.1 cm
Gallery Moos, Toronto
Photography: Art Gallery of
Ontario, Toronto
p. 78

39 *Landscape* 1954
oil on Masonite
27.9 × 36.5 cm
Gallery Moos, Toronto
Photography: Art Gallery of
Ontario, Toronto
p. 79

40 *Parry Sound* 1954
oil on board
40.6 × 50.8 cm
Gallery Moos, Toronto
Photography: Art Gallery of
Ontario, Toronto
p. 79

41 *Midnight* 1955
oil on board
60.5 × 69.7 cm
Gallery Moos, Toronto
Photography: Art Gallery of
Ontario, Toronto
p. 80

42 *Parry Sound No 1* 1955
water-colour
22.9 × 30.5 cm
Gallery Moos, Toronto
Photography: Art Gallery of
Ontario, Toronto
p. 82

43 *Parry Sound No 2* 1955
water-colour
22.9 × 30.5 cm
Gallery Moos, Toronto
Photography: Art Gallery of
Ontario, Toronto
p. 83

44 *Parry Sound No 3* 1955
water-colour
22.9 × 30.5 cm
Gallery Moos, Toronto
Photography: Art Gallery of
Ontario, Toronto
p. 84

45 *Parry Sound No 4* 1955
water-colour
22.9 × 30.5 cm
Gallery Moos, Toronto
Photography: Art Gallery of
Ontario, Toronto
p. 85

46 *Swirling Night* 1955
oil on canvas laid on board
20.3 × 25.4 cm
Hana Trefelt, Toronto
Photography: Art Gallery of
Ontario, Toronto
p. 86

47 *Autumn Skies* 1955
oil on canvas laid on board
25.4 × 35.6 cm
Gallery Moos, Toronto
Photography: Art Gallery of
Ontario, Toronto
p. 86

48 *Dusk* 1955
oil on board
27.3 × 21.6 cm
Gallery Moos, Toronto
Photography: Art Gallery of
Ontario, Toronto
p. 87

49 Iskowitz in Spadina Avenue studio,
1981
Photography: Doron Rescheff,
Toronto
p. 91

50 *Spring* 1962
felt pen
12.5 × 50.2 cm
Gallery Moos, Toronto
p. 96

51 *Untitled drawing* 1958
felt pen
56 × 42.8 cm
Gallery Moos, Toronto
p. 101

52 *Western Sphere No 11* 1969
water-colour
47 × 62 cm
The Canada Council Art Bank,
Ottawa
Photography: John Evans, Ottawa
p. 119

53 *Sky Blue No 3* 1971
oil on canvas
76.2 × 112 cm
Dr and Mrs A.N. Lofchy, Toronto
Photography: Art Gallery of
Ontario, Toronto
p. 122

54 *Uplands E* 1971
oil on canvas
228.6 × 355.6 cm (diptych)
National Gallery of Canada, Ottawa
p. 125

55 *Ultra Blue Green* 1973
oil on canvas
157.6 × 127 cm
Gallery Moos, Toronto
Photography: Art Gallery of
Ontario, Toronto
p. 133

56 *Spring* 1974
oil on canvas
153 × 137.5 cm
The Canada Council Art Bank,
Ottawa
Photography: John Evans, Ottawa
p. 133

57 *Highlands No 2* 1975–76
oil on canvas
216 × 387 cm (diptych)
The Canada Council Art Bank,
Ottawa
Photography: John Evans, Ottawa
p. 140

58 *Variations on Deep Blues
No 3* 1975–76
oil on canvas
223.5 × 355.6 cm (diptych)
The Montreal Museum of Fine Arts,
Montreal
Horsley and Annie Townsend
Bequest
p. 140

59 *Midnight Blue No 7* 1976
oil on canvas
140 × 120 cm
Gerald W. Schwartz, Winnipeg
Photography: Ernest Mayer,
Winnipeg
p. 140

60 *Deep Lilac No 2* 1977
oil on canvas
106.5 × 96.5 cm
Dr and Mrs Paul Chapnick, Toronto
Photography: Art Gallery of
Ontario, Toronto
p. 148

61 *Orange Painting No 1* 1977
oil on canvas
104 × 101.6 cm
Gulf Canada Limited, Calgary
Photography: John Dean, Calgary
p. 149

62 *Lilac C* 1978
oil on canvas
96.5 × 81 cm
The Canada Council Art Bank,
Ottawa
Photography: Ernest Mayer,
Winnipeg
p. 152

63 *Untitled drawing* 1980
felt pen
48 × 62 cm
Mr and Mrs David Anderson,
Buffalo
Photography: T.E. Moore, Toronto
p. 157

64 *Untitled drawing* 1980
felt pen
48 × 62 cm
Mr and Mrs David Anderson
Photography: T.E. Moore, Toronto
p. 157

65 *Untitled drawing* 1980
felt pen
48 × 62 cm
Gallery Moos, Toronto
Photography: T.E. Moore, Toronto
p. 157

66 *Untitled drawing* 1980
felt pen
48 × 62 cm
Gallery Moos, Toronto
Photography: T.E. Moore, Toronto
p. 157

67 Iskowitz in front of Tecumseh Street
studio, 1981
Photography: Doron Rescheff,
Toronto
p. 158

(Back cover flap)
Adele Freedman 1979
felt pen
42.5 × 35 cm
Adele Freedman, Toronto

(Back cover)
Self Portrait 1980
felt pen
41.5 × 34 cm
Gallery Moos, Toronto

In some cases, the dates on paintings and drawings do not agree with
dates given in the captions. The reason for this is that Iskowitz reworked
and re-dated some of his early paintings.

INDEX

DESIGN
The Dragon's Eye Press
PRODUCTION
Paula Chabanais Productions
TYPESETTING
University of Toronto Press
and Word for Word inc.
FILM
Prolith Inc. and
M.P. Graphic Consultants Ltd.
LITHOGRAPHY
Ashton-Potter Ltd
BINDING
The Hunter Rose Company Limited